CASE STUDIES IN
CULTURAL ANTHROPOLOGY

GENERAL EDITORS
George and Louise Spindler
STANFORD UNIVERSITY

THE KALINGA OF NORTHERN LUZON, PHILIPPINES

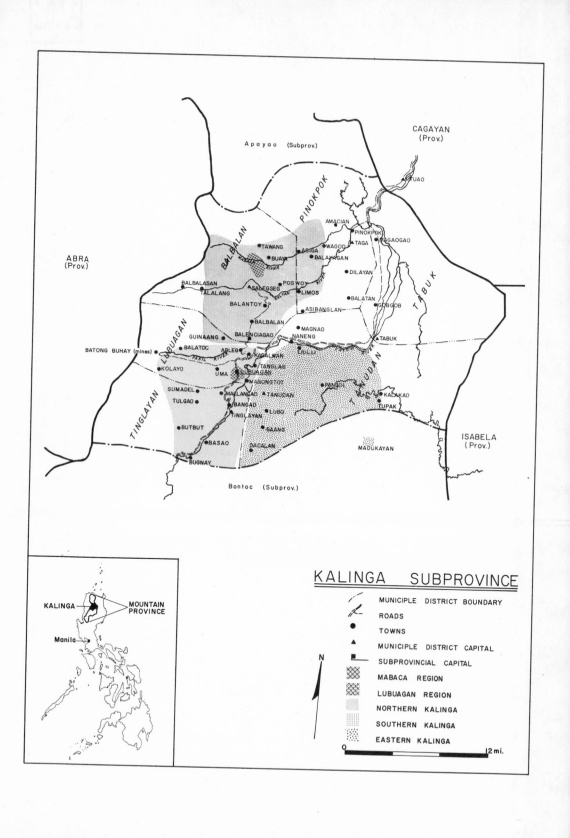

CAGAYAN
(Prov.)

Apayao (Subprov.)

ABRA
(Prov.)

ISABELA
(Prov.)

Bontoc (Subprov.)

BATONG BUHAY (mines)

PINOKPOK

BALBALAN

LUBUAGAN

TINGLAYAN

TABUK

TINGUUDAN

ATUAO

AMACIAN

PINOKPOK
WAGOD   TAGA   MAGAOGAO
TAWANG   ASIGA   BALAWAGAN
BUAYA
DILAYAN
POSWOY
BALBALASAN   SALEGSEG   LIMOS
TALALANG   BALATAN
BALANTOY   GOBGOB
ASIBANGLAN
BALBALAN
MAGNAO
GUINAANG   BALENCIAGAO   NANENG   TABUK
BALATOC   ABLEG   KAGALWAN   DULID
KOLAYO   UMA   TANGLAB
LUBUAGAN
MABONGTOT
SUMADEL   MALANGAO   TANUDAN   PANGOL   KALAKAD
TULGAO   BANGAD   TUPAK
LUBO
BUTBUT   TINGLAYAN   SAANG
BASAO   DACALAN
BUGNAY   MADUKAYAN

KALINGA   SUBPROVINCE

MUNICIPLE DISTRICT BOUNDARY
ROADS
TOWNS
MUNICIPLE DISTRICT CAPITAL
SUBPROVINCIAL CAPITAL
MABACA REGION
LUBUAGAN REGION
NORTHERN KALINGA
SOUTHERN KALINGA
EASTERN KALINGA

N

0   12 mi.

KALINGA   MOUNTAIN
PROVINCE

Manila

THE KALINGA OF NORTHERN LUZON, PHILIPPINES

By

EDWARD P. DOZIER

The University of Arizona

HOLT, RINEHART AND WINSTON

NEW YORK   CHICAGO   SAN FRANCISCO   TORONTO   LONDON

Acknowledgment

We wish to thank the University of Arizona Press for permission to quote from the author's book Mountain Arbiters *(copyright, 1966).*

Library of Congress Catalog Card Number: 67–18877

2641553

Printed in the United States of America

1 2 3 4 5 6 7 8 9

Foreword

About the Series

These case studies in cultural anthropology are designed to bring to students, in beginning and intermediate courses in the social sciences, insights into the richness and complexity of human life as it is lived in different ways and in different places. They are written by men and women who have lived in the societies they write about and who are professionally trained as observers and interpreters of human behavior. The authors are also teachers, and in writing their books they have kept the students who will read them foremost in their minds. It is our belief that when an understanding of ways of life very different from one's own is gained, abstractions and generalizations about social structure, cultural values, subsistence techniques, and the other universal categories of human social behavior become meaningful.

About the Author

The Mountain Province, northern Luzon, Philippines, represents a new area of research for Edward P. Dozier. A native of Santa Clara Pueblo, New Mexico, Dr. Dozier is widely known for his work in the Southwest, particularly on the Pueblo Indians of Arizona and New Mexico. He has published numerous articles in linguistic and anthropological journals. Another case study, *Hano: A Tewa Indian Community in Arizona,* was published in 1966 by Holt, Rinehart and Winston, Inc. The University of Arizona Press published a more extensive report of the author's investigations among the Kalinga in 1966 under the title: *Mountain Arbiters—The Changing Life of a Philippine Hill People.*

Dr. Dozier received his Ph.D. from the University of California at Los Angeles, taught at the University of Oregon and Northwestern University, and is now professor of anthropology at the University of Arizona. In 1958–1959 he was a Fellow at the Center for Advanced Studies in the Behavioral Sciences at Stanford, California. He is a member of the board of directors for the Association on American Indian Affairs and a Fellow of the American Association for the Advancement of Science and the American Anthropological Association.

About the Book

Headhunting was not long ago the major occupation of able-bodied Kalinga males and the major basis of prestige, besides oratorical ability, among them.

Today, both headhunting and warfare are controlled by peace pacts between various regions of the Kalinga territory. These pacts are initiated and maintained by the Kalinga themselves, and use established Kalinga mechanisms of communication and decision-making. Dr. Dozier provides detailed case materials on each step of the development of a peace pact, from the first exchanges between individuals to the level of regional involvement. He shows how the negotiations provide an arena for the skilled leader and orator, how these negotiations in themselves provide a rechanneling of the headhunting functions, and how they are characteristic Kalinga institutions. Negotiations are always touch and go since the Kalinga are very sensitive to insult and demand reparations when they occur, so negotiations are frequently interrupted by interludes of music and dancing to divert protagonists. The dry season, which was once the headhunting season, is now the time of peace pact celebrations, when feasting and dancing, as well as oratory and debate, are featured. In general, the interregional peace pacts contain specific provision for such matters as delineation of boundaries, settlement of killings or woundings, stealing, guarantees of hospitality to visitors and traders, and respect for the neutral status of given regions in their relations with one another.

This case study does not overemphasize the more spectacular aspects of Kalinga life at the expense of others. Dr. Dozier provides careful discussion of kinship groups, the major of which is the kinship circle. Attention is given to relationships within this circle, such as grandparent-grandchild, which is particularly affectionate among Kalinga; parent-child, which is more on the practical side; and those of children with uncles and aunts, to whom they often go when punished or in some difficulty with their parents. The author also gives a particularly good account of the rituals, observances, and major events of the life cycle from birth to death. There is in addition a summary of religion and ritualistic activity. The author points out parallels to Kalinga temporal life, showing how the principles of vengeance, appeasement, and generosity which operate in the everyday life of the Kalinga also characterize the behavior of supernaturals and their relations with mortals.

GEORGE AND LOUISE SPINDLER
General Editors

Stanford, California
January 1967

Preface

Most of the data for this report are based on fieldwork among the Northern Kalinga particularly in the regions of Mabaca and Poswoy. Comparative materials from the Southern Kalinga are drawn primarily from the scholarly study of the Lubuagan Kalinga by F. R. Barton (1949). In all, a period of one year was spent among the Kalinga from July 1959 to July 1960. Continuous residence in a single hamlet or town was no longer than a month. To understand the broad patterns of Kalinga life, a field researcher must cover considerable territory in an extremely rugged and mountainous terrain. The scattered residence pattern which disperses families of a kindred into different hamlets brings about considerable mobility of the regional population. Individuals and families frequently visit one another and attend feasts associated with the life cycle. During the dry season mobility is accentuated and travel is extended interregionally; anywhere from three to ten peace pact celebrations might be visited over a period of three months by the Kalinga themselves. To share as much as possible in Kalinga life, I became a part of this pattern of mobility and went along with the Kalinga to regional festivals and the popular interregional peace pact celebrations.

The Kalinga are not culturally homogeneous. There is considerable variation from region to region and the differences become pronounced with distance. Yet despite these variations, general patterns are shared across regional boundaries and spill over into neighboring provinces and subprovinces. Certainly, of all the peoples in the Mountain Province bearing ethnic designations, the Kalinga have the most compelling sense of tribal awareness. This is a recent phenomenon and largely the result of the Kalinga peace pact institution, which brings Kalinga from near and distant parts of the subprovince together.

A senior postdoctoral fellowship from the National Science Foundation made possible my field research, and upon my return to the States, an American Philosophical Society grant-in-aid permitted me to organize my field materials. To both of these institutions I am extremely grateful. My initial interest in the Mountain Province was triggered by stimulating discussions with Fred and Dorothy Eggan, who subsequently lent moral and professional support to my field studies. Many Kalinga, too numerous to single out for special recognition, assisted me in many ways to get to know them. Their friendship and aid is generously acknowledged. For help in the field and in writing this report, I am most grateful to my wife, Marianne Fink Dozier, who supplied me liberally with constructive criticism and constant encouragement.

Edward P. Dozier

Tucson, Arizona
January 1967

Contents

Foreword   v

Preface   vii

Introduction   1

1. Social Organization and Social Life   10

    Territorial and Social Units, 10
    Cultural Subdivisions, 10
    The Region, 12
    Villages and Hamlets, 15
    Household and Extended Household, 17
    The Kinship Circle or Kindred and the
      Bilateral Descent Group, 20
    The Kinship System, 23
      Key Features of the Terminology, 24
      Kinship Behavior, 25
      Grandparent-Grandchildren, 25
      Parent-Child Relationship, 26
      Uncles and Aunts, Nephews and Nieces, 28
      Siblings and Cousins, 29
      Affinal or In-Law Relations, 29

2. From Birth to Death   32

    Pregnancy and Birth, 32
    The Kontad Ceremonies: Infancy and
      Early Years, 36
    Later Childhood, 39
    Contract Marriages, 41
    Uncontracted Marriages, 44
    Mistresses, 45
    Divorce, 46
    Adult Life and Occupational Activities, 47
    Illness, 52
    Funeral Rites, 52

3. Religion—Ritual and Beliefs   55

    Religious Concepts, 55
    Categories of Ritualistic Activity, 58
    The Medium and the Placation of
       Spirits, 59
    The Nature of Kalinga Religion, 62
    Western and Christian Influences, 64

4. Warfare and Headhunting   67

    Warfare, 68
    Headhunting, 69

5. The Peace Pact Institution   82

6. Social and Cultural Reorganization   98

References   100

Recommended Reading   102

Introduction

THE KALINGA are one of several ethnolinguistic peoples inhabiting the mountainous terrain of northern Luzon. The lifeway of all these groups was formerly marked by feuds, warfare, and frequent headhunting forays. Since the turn of the century, head-taking has subsided, but occasional killings sparked by old feuds still occur. Among the Kalinga, the incidence of homicide and warefare has been lowered, primarily by appeal to formal peace pacts. Western influences, particularly the introduction of modern firearms, changed the whole complexion of traditional warfare and headhunting practices. The spear and the head axe kept casualties low, but warfare with repeating rifles threatened wholesale slaughter. The situation which the feuding Kalinga regional populations faced in the latter part of the nineteenth century was not unlike the genocidal holocaust confronting the world today. If the mountain populations were not to be drastically reduced, some alternative for settling disputes had to be found. The Kalinga's answer was the peace pact institution. Roy F. Barton, one of the first serious scholars of the mountain peoples, made a study of Kalinga custom law and social institutions (Barton 1949). He characterized the peace pact institution, in association with the territorial regional unit of the Kalinga, as an international device for negotiating, securing and maintaining peace. Barton also considered the Kalinga to be a step beyond the tribal level—a group emerging into a state organization. The latter observation may be an exaggeration, for kinship principles predominate in Kalinga thinking and behavior. Nevertheless, the peace pact institution, as an instrument for diminishing the incidence of headhunting and settling interregional troubles, has been highly effective. Peace pacts have spread rapidly throughout the Kalinga subprovince and even bind groups in neighboring subprovinces. In addition to keeping peace, the festivals which occur in connection with the establishment of new pacts and the frequent renewals of old ones serve social and recreational functions. The Kalinga now travel extensively and the existence of peace pacts over a wide area insures food, lodging, and generous hospitality for travelers. The details of the peace pact institution will be discussed in a special section of this report.

1

Rice cultivation is basic to all the mountain peoples. The groups centrally located in the area subsist on wet rice. Classic among wet-rice farmers are the Bontoc and the Ifugao, who grow rice on elaborate rice terraces climbing up steep mountain slopes for hundreds of feet. Irrigated rice terraces appear to be new among the Kalinga, whose territory joins that of the Bontoc and Ifugao on the north. The Kalinga use both wet- and dry-rice techniques; those nearest the Bontoc and Ifugao grow rice on irrigated terraces, while those in the northern and eastern marginal areas grow rice on hill and mountain sides by slash-and-burn techniques. Even in these remote areas, however, irrigated terraces are coming in with the expansion of the population (Scott 1958a).

Shortly after the Philippines came under American rule, the mountain peoples were incorporated under a separate province—the Mountain Province. The province was then divided into subprovinces roughly corresponding to the enthnolinguistic groups occupying the area. From south to north these subprovinces are as follows: Benguet, Bontoc, Ifugao, Kalinga, and Apayao. The last four groups are also the names of ethnolinguistic groups, but the subprovince of Benguet contains two ethnolinguistic peoples, the Ibaloy and Kankanay. Outside the Mountain Province, in the eastern sector of the province of Abra, live another important ethnolinguistic group, the Tinguian. This last group has close cultural affinities to the Kalinga and the Isneg or Apayao. In recent years the populations in the subprovinces have begun to develop a sense of ethnic identity, but everywhere the community or local region continues to be the basic social unit. There are linguistic variations from community to community, but there are no sharp breaks from one local region to another. The same is true for the distribution of cultural complexes. The extremes exhibit pronounced differences in both dialect and culture, but from one community to its nearest neighbor, differences are slight. The materials from which this report is drawn come primarily from the northern Kalinga area, but to give the description of the Kalinga unity and consistency, general patterns rather than differences have been emphasized.

The southern and central parts of the Mountain Province have the highest elevations and represent the most rugged mountain features. Toward the north and northeast the mountains are lower and end abruptly on the north coast and the Cagayan Valley. The Kalinga country is most rugged in the south where the Chico, the main river of the province, bisects Bontoc and Kalinga subprovinces. The ridges on either side of the Chico rise to heights of 5000 and 6000 feet. Characteristic vegetation on the tops of the ridges is pine, with cogon grass on the steep slopes and semitropical and tropical growth in the river valleys, where groves of coconut trees mark the settlements. The lower levels, where most of the villages are located, vary between 1500 and 2000 feet in elevation. The Chico River swings in wide arcs in this area before turning sharply northeastward toward the Cagayan Valley. The arcs of the river and the rapid lateral streams have formed slopes which are gentler than the Bontoc country further south. Here the Kalinga have terraced the slopes into rich rice fields, although the terraces do not achieve the engineering excellence of those of the Bontoc and Ifugao. Kalinga terraces are not held back by vertical retaining walls but slope gently at an angle.

A newly constructed rice paddy in the Mabaca region (northern Kalinga).

The northern and eastern Kalinga areas are also mountainous—not so high as the southern portion of the Mountain Province, but areas of high sierras, steep mountainsides, and deep canyons. The typical vegetation is a tropical or subtropical rain forest, thick in the narrow valleys but often bare on the mountain slopes where the people have burned the verdant growth to cultivate upland rice and sugarcane. Irrigated rice fields are new in the area and appear only where the topography easily lends itself to terracing.

Like other Philippine provinces, the Mountain Province has been divided into a number of municipalities. The subprovince of Kalinga has six municipal districts: Tinglayan, Lubuagan, Tanudan, Balbalan, Pinokpok, and Tabuk. The most densely populated area of indigenous Kalinga people is the Lubuagan municipal district, where the 1960 census gave a total figure of 10,266. The barrio, or region, of Lubuagan, consisting of some fifteen closely clustered towns and hamlets, contains about 4000 people, almost half of the total municipal population. The other municipal districts of Kalinga subprovince indicated populations in the 1960 census as follows: Tinglayan, 9120; Tanudan, 4595; Balbalan, 7529; Pinokpok, 7037; and Tabuk, 21,235. The Tabuk municipal district has experienced a large influx of lowland immigrants in recent years, and it would be difficult to determine what proportion of the population is specifically Kalinga. The total Kalinga population of the subprovince of Kalinga and the populations of the neighboring areas considered to be Kalinga is now generally estimated at around 40,000.

Settlement patterns in the northern and eastern margins of the Kalinga subprovince differ markedly from those in the south. In the northern areas the clusterings of houses are small hamlets consisting of half a dozen to no more than thirty houses. In the south, particularly in the municipalities of Lubuagan and Tinglayan, the settlements are considerably larger and may properly be called towns. The town of Mabilong in the Lubuagan region, for example, consists of 254 houses with a population of 1248. Moreover, Mabilong is contiguous with several other towns forming the municipal center of Lubuagan with a population of almost 4000. This is also true of settlements in the Tinglayan municipal district where, for example, Bangad and Tinglayan proper each have several hundred houses and more than 1000 inhabitants.

While dwellings differ considerably within one village, and even more radically between distant sectors of the Kalinga country, we may hazard a few general statements about them. All houses are raised above the ground on posts, with steps or a ladder leading up to a single entrance. The majority of the houses are square or rectangular single-room dwellings. The walls are commonly made either of split and plaited bamboo or handhewn planks. In the more traditional homes the floors are of split-bamboo mats which rest on a grating of small beams. The mats are removable and are taken to a nearby stream two or three times a week and thoroughly washed before being returned to the house. Each dwelling has a fire pit set a little off center and toward the back of the floor. The fire pit is a square box about a yard wide and 4 to 6 inches high, filled with sand and accumulated ash. Above the fire pit is a rack for drying wood, food, or wearing apparel. Roofs are pitched, made of runo reeds and thatched with cogon grass.

Mount Makelkelon, a prominent land feature of the northern Kalinga area.

In every hamlet or town there are at least one or more houses with galvanized pitched roofs with floors and walls of handhewn boards. Occasionally such houses have a second house of traditional construction, either connected to the main house or situated nearby, which is used as a kitchen. These new-style houses are predominant in some towns and hamlets and will undoubtedly replace the typical native thatch-roofed houses of traditional construction in the near future.

Community life is similar in all the Kalinga areas I have visited. Women and children are most in evidence around the village. Babies are rarely put down but are carried by mother, father, aunts, or sisters in blanket slings. The blanket is passed over one shoulder and tied in front, while the baby rides on the back or on either hip comfortably supported by the blanket. For a mother with a nursing child, the baby is simply slung around to the front when it wishes to suckle. A woman carrying a baby in a blanket sling goes about her work seemingly unhampered, transporting heavy loads poised on her head, winnowing rice, cooking and performing a myriad of other household tasks while the baby observes the world about it or naps peacefully under the rocking motion.

Dogs, pigs, and chickens roam at will about the village. The barking of dogs at night may be disturbing to an unaccustomed visitor, but if he must spend any time in a Kalinga village, he must adjust to it or get no sleep at all. The visitor who is offended by roaming pigs should keep away from Kalinga towns and hamlets. These creatures, from the newly born to huge brutes, are everywhere. A grunting sow with suckling young lying contentedly underneath a house or in the proximity of playing, naked children is a typical village sight. The carabao, or water buffalo, is rarely seen in the village but commonly in the outskirts of the settlement or in rice fields, either at work or wallowing happily in a pool of water or puddle of mud.

The dress of the Kalinga in the upper Saltan and Mabaca River Valleys differs in many respects from the Kalinga of the Chico Valley. Differences were more pronounced early in this century, but there are still some significant differences at present. Formerly, in what is now the northern Balbalan district and the whole of Pinokpok district, the Kalinga dressed themselves in brightly colored cotton fabrics. Worcester (1913:1213) describes the dress of these Kalinga as follows:

> The men wear regulation clouts, but they are not seldom ornamented with beads, buttons, etc. Their short jackets of gaudily colored cloth are also often adorned with beads and tassels. Gay turbans are commonly worn, and their hair, banged across the forehead and left long behind, is frequently stuck full of scarlet hibiscus, marigolds and other gay flowers and of really gorgeous feather ornaments. Handsome blankets worn over one shoulder and under the opposite arm and ornamental bags for carrying small personal belongings complete the usual costume of the male, except for the ear plugs, which are fashioned with especial care and are often inserted in such a way as to project backward against the sides of the neck and turn the lobes of the ears directly forward. Their front ends are covered with embroidered cloth or adorned with highly polished coins, bits of looking-glass, or other bright objects. In some instances the ear plugs are made of rolls of brightly colored worsted.

A southern Kalinga family from the Bugnay-Butbut region. Note the difference in dress between these people and those from northern Kalinga.

A Kalinga woman from Limos (northern Kalinga) dressed in the typical northern Kalinga fashion. Strands of agate-bead necklaces and bead and/or brass bracelets on lower arms are worn by both northern and southern Kalinga women on festive occasions.

The women wear gaily colored upper garments and skirts. The wealthier ones have enormous necklaces of agate beads, while heavy and peculiarly shaped ear ornaments of brass and of mother-of-pearl are almost invariably in evidence. Their heads are adorned not only with abundant natural locks, but with switches made from the tresses of departed female ancestors or of relatives having long hair. Into the masses of hair thus built up are thrust gay scarlet and yellow feather plumes.

The dress of the Southern Kalinga in the present municipal district of Lubuagan and Tinglayan was more simple and subdued in color. Men wore their hair long in back and banged in front as the Northern Kalinga, but decorations and garments were at a minimum. The G-string was like that of the Kalinga of the northern regions, but commonly the upper body was bare, although tattooed if the man had participated in a killing. A choker of agate beads was also worn, and sometimes a basket hat like that worn by the Bontocs but decorated with beads. Women wore simply the wraparound skirt (*tapis*), while the upper part of the body was left bare. Occasionally a sort of bustle made of woven rattan was worn under the skirt, apparently to enhance the charms of the wearer. The arms were tattooed from just below the elbow to the shoulders and sometimes in an area just above the breasts. Some women, especially unmarried, postadolescent girls, also painted their faces with a red pigment. Strands of agate-bead necklaces and occasionally bead wristlets completed the costume.

The influx of lowland Filipinos and Christian influences have modified the traditional dress of the Kalinga, more in the north than in the south but generally throughout Kalinga land. The colorful costume of the Northern Kalinga has been replaced for women by the American-style cotton dress. Men wear trousers or trousers cut into shorts and either nothing above the waist or an old shirt. G-strings for men and the *tapis* for women are seldom in evidence anymore among the Northern Kalinga.

The Kalinga in the Lubuagan and Tinglayan districts adhere to traditional costumes much more faithfully. Women are more often bare above the waist and perhaps the majority prefer the native wraparound skirt. Men, too, are more frequently seen wearing the traditional G-string. The agate necklace beads are also more consistently worn by the Kalinga women of the south, although the men in both areas wear the agate-bead chokers only in native dances or to have their pictures taken.

Feuds and occasional killings characterize the Kalinga in the south (especially in the Tinglayan district); hence men who travel away from their barrios are well armed with headaxes and spears. Weapons are rarely seen in the north where the feuding pattern has virtually disappeared. Undoubtedly adherence to traditional dress is part of a complex of cultural conservatism among the Southern Kalinga. Feuds and revenge killings are important ingredients in this complex. We will discuss this topic in greater detail later on.

Activities revolving around the principal crop, rice, are always in evidence. The rhythmic sound of pounding rice is heard from early in the morning until late in the evening. Virtually at any time during the day one may see the transporting of *palay* (unthreshed rice) in baskets on the balanced pole by men or in baskets posed on the heads of women. An equally typical sight is that of women ascending from a nearby brook with water jars stacked on their heads. All activities go on in an atmosphere of unrestrained chatter and laughter.

Life is safer and more secure today than in the past. Through Western influence and acculturation, most of the Kalinga are exchanging headhunting and the anxieties of warfare for a system of peace pacts and a consequent preoccupation with politics. Kalinga regional leaders (*pangat*) and outstanding warriors (*mangol*) now arbitrate regional and interregional disputes, matching oratorical wits with one another.* On a municipal, subprovincial and provincial level these men vie for elective political positions. The Kalinga thus are satisfying the same drive for individual distinction that in the past made them take to spear and headaxe.

---

* Kalinga native words have been simplified and rendered in Roman letters. For a more exact phonetic transcription see the author's *Mountain Arbiters: The Changing Life of a Philippine Hill People*. University of Arizona Press, 1966.

Social Organization and Social Life

Kalinga Territorial and Social Units

THE FOLLOWING describes both the territorial and the social units which have past and present significance to the Kalinga themselves. These units are as follows: cultural subdivisions, the region, villages and hamlets, household and extended household, the kinship circle or kindred, and the bilateral descent group. None of these entities are formally recognized by the Philippine government as administrative units. The territorial units which now directly affect the Kalinga—the municipal districts, the subprovince, the province, and the Philippine nation—were unknown in the past. A Kalinga cultural universe roughly coterminous with the boundary lines of the present subprovince is recognized by the Kalinga. The primary reason for this has been the linguistic and cultural affinities shared by all the Kalinga and the spread of the popular peace pacts. The Kalinga as an ethnolinguistic group was never a political unit, however. There was no organization beyond the kinship group, except the peace pact institution which is not an instrument of political federation. Since the formation of the Mountain Province and its subprovinces in 1907, the Kalinga have been developing a kind of tribal consciousness, but this identity is not strong (Scott 1960:243).

Kalinga Cultural Subdivisions

Three subcultural areas among the Kalinga are evident to anyone who has visited the Kalinga and neighboring subprovinces. These cultural subdivisions are geographical and may be simply designated as the southern, northern, and eastern Kalinga areas. The Kalinga themselves are cognizant of these divisions and frequently refer to the social and cultural characteristics of each subdivision. In a sense there are as many distinctive subcultures as there are regions and the Kalinga tend to think of differences in this way. The home region is where one has relatives and where one's loyalties are anchored. The feeling is still strong that people from other regions, whether Kalinga or not, are not to be trusted. This is of course a reflection of past conditions when anyone from another region was an enemy and hence fair game if found trespassing. Circumstances have changed and the peace pact institution protects the life of a member of another region and extends to such a person the same privileges as a regional member. Yet if the peace pact is broken, conditions revert back to the past and the life of a person from a region with which a pact has been severed is in danger until the pact is reinstated. Thus, conditions of the past, when regional populations were hostile to one another, still pervade the thinking of the Kalinga.

While the peace pact is definitely a recent device to overcome interregional hostilities, other mechanisms were used occasionally to bring neighboring regional members together. A trading partnership between men of two different regions is quite widespread in the Philippines and is obviously an old type of relationship. This relationship protected the traders and members of their families from harm when in one another's regions. Occasionally such contacts resulted in interregional marriages and hence provided the basis for considerable social and cultural exchange. It is understandable, therefore, that despite interregional hostilities, those regions which occupied a contiguous territory had greater contact with one another than did those regions remote from one another and separated by formidable geographical barriers. The three subcultural divisions of the Kalinga are of this kind; they are delimited from one another by prominent geographical features, while inside each subdivision geographical barriers are minimal.

The northern and southern Kalinga areas are rather sharply divided by an east-west river, the Pacil, which is fairly large and runs a considerable distance of its course in a deep gorge.

The eastern Kalinga area is perhaps the most isolated from a geographical standpoint. The high ridge running north and south parallel to the Chico River separates this area from the Southern Kalinga. The northern and eastern Kalinga subcultural areas are separated partly by the southern Kalinga area which intervenes between them, and farther north by the Chico River. Since the American period, the Eastern Kalinga along the Tanudan River, across the ridge from the Chico and running parallel to it, have had considerable intercourse with the Southern Kalinga and a number of marriages have taken place between the two groups. As the result of these circumstances, the Tanudan River Kalinga and the Southern Kalinga are perhaps not as distinctively apart culturally as each is from the northern Kalinga area.

An interesting group of nomadic Kalinga are reported in the eastern part of the present Tanudan municipal district, the Kalakad-Tupak regions. This group may well form a fourth major subcultural area of the Kalinga. Little is known of these people even by other Kalinga. These Kalinga are in touch with the Eastern Kalinga and have extended peace pact relations with them. The Kalakad-Tupak Kalinga are reported to live primarily on wild fruits, hunt and defend themselves with the bow and arrow, and live in tree houses. Until more information is gath-

ered about this group, however, we cannot identify them as a separate cultural enti-
ty.

It is relevant here to call attention to another group of Kalinga, the Madukayan. This group of Kalinga was reported to have a population of 359 in the
1948 Philippine census and occupies a barrio of the same name in the municipal
district of Natonin, Bontoc. They are migrants from the Tanudan Valley, however,
and are culturally and linguistically Eastern Kalinga (Scott 1958b:318–319).

Along the margins of the three major cultural areas delimited here,
influences of outside cultural groups are evident. Thus among the Isneg in the
north, the Bontoc in the south, and in the northcentral portion of the Kalinga subprovince, Ilocano pressures from the province of Cagayan and Tinguian influence
from the province of Abra have all left their cultural imprint on the Kalinga. Yet
each area exhibits internal uniformity in dialects, in dress and adornment, and
somewhat in architecture, although house types tend to be rather variable even
within a single village (Anderson 1960; Vanoverbergh 1929; Scott 1962).

The Region

The largest geographical unit recognized as a social unit by the Kalinga is
the region. Northern Kalinga refer to the region in their dialect as *boboloy,* but in
speaking with outsiders they use the term barrio or tribe. Regions differ in size,
with apparently available food sources, population densities and the strength and
prowess of neighboring regions imposing limitations. The Lubuagan region in the
more densely populated southern area has a diameter of approximately 4 miles,
whereas in the sparsely populated northern area, Mabaca has a diameter roughly of
7 miles. The northern regions today undoubtedly most nearly typify past conditions. Here, populations are small and dispersed in hamlets. In the Mabaca region
the settlements are scattered over an area of about 40 square miles. The largest of
these, Canao Norte, has only forty-one houses closely clustered together. There
were thirteen settlements designated by name in Mabaca at the time of my visit.
These ranged from forty-one houses to one (see Tables 1 and 2).

Informants report considerable shifting of the settlements; former hamlets
have been abandoned, others reduced to a single house or two, while new ones
have been founded. The nature of the subsistence economy, dry-rice agriculture,
undoubtedly accounts for frequent changes of habitation, but safety precautions
have also brought about relocations of settlements. Dwellings are characteristically
located on leveled areas on the slopes of steep mountains where the view is unob-
structed or else in isolated pockets in deep canyons. Until recently, villages were
stockaded, and along the trails approaching the village were carefully concealed
pits at the bottom of which were sharpened bamboos ready to catch and maim or
kill the unwary stranger. Deadfalls in the form of an overhanging or leaning heavy
log to be tripped by a string across the trail were designed to kill a stranger or
warn the village of his approach. Only the members of the region knew the location of such traps and warning devices.

TABLE 1

A TERRITORIAL REGION IN THE SOUTH KALINGA AREA:
THE LUBUAGAN REGION

(Population based on 1959 figures obtained in the municipal office)

Town or Hamlet	Houses	Population
Lubuagan *población* (contiguous villages or wards)		
Linas	122	625
Kimatan	47	229
Balili	54	303
Tiwod	33	172
Gotgotong	13	56
Mabilong (contiguous villages or wards)		
Mabilong proper	254	1248
Gongogong	31	124
Dugnac	70	320
Manangol	20	105
Doy-as	23	134
Dang-oy (contiguous villages or wards)		
Upper Dang-oy	47	261
Lower Dang-oy	33	154
Ga-ang	54	141
Tabangao	18	77
Agsiang	10	51
Totals	839	4000

Persons per house 4.8

TABLE 2

A TERRITORIAL REGION IN THE NORTH KALINGA AREA:
THE MABACA REGION

(Population based on a house and population count made in 1959)

Hamlet	Houses	Population
Canao	41	224
Cawayan (site of school house) ⎫		
Tappo ⎪		
Bocay ⎬	19	102
Dapo-og ⎪		
Masa-it ⎭		
Danogdog ⎫		
Pasna-an ⎬	9	48
Calcatan ⎭		
Balala	12	88
Madalit	13	71
Agodong ⎫		
Bayowong ⎭	18	79
Totals	112	612

Persons per house: 5.5

It is quite clear that in the past, region and kinship circle (see below) were equated in the thinking of the people. Actually, equating the kinship group with an endogamous region has not disappeared. Peace pacts, for example, are thought to be between kinship groups rather than between areas (Barton 1949:174). In the north and in certain isolated areas of the south, regional populations are small; hence, the theory of equating kinship group with region may sometimes accord with fact. Populations of the regions in the north, the region of Salegseg excepted, are about 500, whereas in the south, the norm is about 1000, with the Lubuagan region alone having a population of 4000 (see population figures). It is virtually impossible in the northern Kalinga regions for an individual not to be related at least within a third cousin degree with every other individual. At present, the Kalinga still operate in terms of the kinship principle, but it is obvious that in the more densely populated regions kinship group and region cannot correspond. In recent years, with expanded populations within the region, greater interregional mobility, and increasing marriages with Kalinga of other regions, the native equation of kinship groups with region is beginning to be modified and as a result, the modern-imposed municipal form of government is beginning to have meaning. But the importance of the region as a sociopolitical unit has not been displaced anywhere in favor of the larger municipal district.

Expanded populations have brought about pressures on cultivatable land and with it, migrations out of home regions and the founding of new colonies. In such cases, the daughter colony for a time remains a political dependency of the parent region. That is, it is considered a part of the parent region and included in all its peace pacts. Uma in 1940 during Barton's study (1949:35) was such a dependency of Lubuagan, but it had already started to break away from the parent region by making a separate peace pact with Balbalasan. At present, Uma is completely independent and makes its own peace pacts with other regions. Other parent-daughter regions are the following: the Tinglayan district—Butbut-Bugnay, Sumadel-Mallango, Sumadel-Kolayo (the daughter colony is in Lubuagan district); the Balbalan district—Pantikian-Balbalasan (called Banao), Poswoy-Daongan-Ababaan, Mabaca-Amacian (daughter colony in Pinokpok district); the Lubugan district—Guinaang-Dalupa-Ableg and the Tanuadan district—Lubo-Gaang.

In the cases above, most peace pacts covering the parent region also extend to the daughter colony or colonies, but the daughter colonies are beginning to make separate peace pacts and they may eventually become completely independent politically from the parent regions. Intermarriage between people of daughter colonies and parent region occur even after political relations have been suspended. This extension of marriage relations to migrant populations is another factor, besides the high mobility of the Kalinga already mentioned, which is contributing to the breakup of the localized, endogamous regions.

A number of Kalinga migrants from different regions of Balbalan district, that is, the northern Kalinga area, have in recent years settled together in various parts of Pinokpok and Tabuk districts, the subprovince of Apayao and the province of Cagayan. Formerly these areas were not occupied by Kalinga for two primary reasons: (1) they were enemy territory, if occupied at all; and (2) the areas were malaria infested. At present, with danger to lives diminished by the peace pact institution and Philippine law enforcement agencies, and the effectiveness of malaria control projects, large numbers of Kalinga and other mountain peoples have migrated into these areas. The Kalinga settlers are for a time protected by the peace pacts of their former home regions but some settlements are now making their own peace pacts with other regions. Some of these new communities are: Amacian in Pinokpok district, mostly Mabaca immigrants (see above); Magaogao, straddling Pinokpok and Tabuk districts; Wagud, Pinokpok district; Mawanan in Apayao; and Balaknit and Tuao in Cagayan. These communities all have peace pacts of their own, while they remain covered by pacts from home for other regions.

Northern Kalinga inhabitants have also founded settlements in the province of Abra. Two of these communities, Buneg and Lakub, have peace pacts with many of the Kalinga regions of the central area.

Expansion in Kalinga population can be correlated with the adoption of a more stable economy in the form of wet rice agriculture, while modern conditions, particularly contact with Western cultures and Christian missionaries, have brought about mobility and friendly interaction among Kalinga of all regions. Basic to free movement for a people formerly living in small groups and in hostile relations with their neighbors of adjacent regions has been the peace pact institution.

Villages and Hamlets

Within each region are a number of villages and hamlets. In the south where the settlements are typically large, the term "barrio" is variously employed both for the region and for the large towns such as Mabilong, Lubuagan and Bangad proper, which are towns within a region having populations numbering several hundred inhabitants. While the region is usually named after its main or largest settlement, as for example the regions of Lubuagan and Bangad, other regions are designated by a name for which there is no settlement. Thus, for example, the regions of Salegseg and Mabaca have no settlements by those names. An individual among the Kalinga everywhere identifies himself as from such-and-such a region, and only when pressed to name the exact place of residence will he designate his town or hamlet specifically. This is because the settlement in which he lives is not an important social unit. To the Kalinga the household, extended household, kinship circle or kindred, and territorial region are the significant units of his society. An individual's household and extended household are localized in a town or hamlet, but his kinship circle or kindred is dispersed throughout the various settlements in his region. And, in the north more consistently than in the south, the kinship circle or kindred is often conceived to be the whole population of the region.

Among the Northern Kalinga, but undoubtedly characteristic of the Kalinga generally in the past, hamlets are never very permanent and there are frequent shiftings of the settlements and reshufflings of the population within the region. Despite such relocations of settlements, kinship ties remain a strong bond; considerable visiting goes on among close kin, and there are numerous occasions on

The Lubuagan region (southern Kalinga). The town of Lubuagan is in the upper right corner of the picture.

A portion of the Mabaca region (northern Kalinga), with the hamlet of Canao in the foreground. The tin-roofed structures are a chapel and a storehouse of the Roman Catholic mission.

which the members of the kinship circle or kindred come together. In the north, where kinship group and region are believed to be coextensive, regional solidarity is strong; but in the south swollen populations within a region have given rise to complicated problems. Whereas feuding and vengeance within a region are practically unknown in the north, in the south such conflicts are of common occurrence. Thus, for example, when I asked a boy in Tangadan, Lubuagan region, to accompany me to Mabilong, a barrio of the same region and only about 50 feet from Tangadan, he begged to be excused. His family explained that he might be the victim of revenge for an unsettled fight several weeks before between two youths, one of whom was a first cousin of the boy. Lubuagan informants report many similar instances and Barton (1949) reported a number of serious disputes and even killings involving kindreds within the region of Lubuagan during the period of his study there in 1940.

The Household and Extended Household

The household is the residence unit among the Kalinga. It is occupied by a nuclear family and perhaps an aged parent or grandparent of one of the spouses. In a few wealthy households, there may also be a servant (*poyong*) or two. The average size of the households in the Lubuagan municipal district in 1959 was 4.5 persons, but for the more densely populated Lubuagan region the average was 4.8. The number of households for the whole of Balbalan district was not available, but a survey of one region, Mabaca, indicated 5.5 persons per household (see Tables 1 and 2). The genealogies from Lubuagan and Mabaca indicated many children (as many as fifteen in some families, although the mean was about seven) born to a family, but only three or four surviving beyond the age of puberty. Mortality below the age of twelve is high and particularly so below the age of three. Diarrhea was given as the chief cause of death in early childhood. The generally unsanitary conditions which surround houses and settlements are, of course, breeding places for disease bacteria of all kinds. The purity of drinking water is never strictly maintained and the inhabitants of a village frequently use the nearest water source, which is often polluted. Pigs roam the village and may be seen wallowing in mud near streams from which drinking water is drawn. When disease epidemics hit a village, the whole population is usually infected since dwellings are clustered together and few precautions are taken to avoid getting the disease.

While the individuals living under one roof are usually restricted to a nuclear family with perhaps an attached dependent relative, economic activities are shared by a larger interacting circle of relatives living in two or more houses located in a common area. This larger unit, varying in size but involving two or more nuclear families, we may designate as the extended household. The maximum number of interacting households from our Lubuagan sample of extended households was four and the mean, three. The range and mean were the same in Mabaca, but in Mabaca more individuals live under one roof (see above). The number of interacting households, especially in Lubuagan, is partly dictated by the number of married daughters, for residence there is predominately uxorilocal (that is, residence near the wife's parents) since the bride's relatives construct a home near the girl's parental home or on land provided by her relatives. Initially, a Lubuagan couple may live temporarily with the wife's parents while their own house is being built, but as soon as their house is ready, they leave the girl's parents' home. Informants in Lubuagan report that residence of this type may be broken down in two ways: (1) if parents have many daughters and they have already provided dwellings for them, then one of the daughters may be permitted to locate in her husband's household area in a house constructed with the aid of relatives of both bride and groom; (2) If the groom's parents are well-to-do and influential and there is obvious advantage in setting up patrilocal residence.

The belief that the bride's parents and relatives should provide the house and house site is strong among both the Southern and Northern Kalinga, but it is especially strong in Lubuagan. A family (and its relatives) which cannot provide a home for its daughters in Lubuagan is shamed. Since loss of face is an extremely powerful negative sanction in Kalinga culture, every effort is made to observe traditional customs.

Among the Northern Kalinga, the matrilocal or uxorilocal residence pattern is less consistently followed. Greater mobility within the region, necessitated by the predominantly shifting form of agricultural practices, results in a more varied form of residence. Although couples most commonly locate near the wife's parents' home (or even move into the same house), there are a number of instances of patrilocal residence and even more of neolocal residence in a hamlet different from either of the parents. A location more convenient to the swidden (dry-rice plot) or rice fields being farmed usually determines the place of residence. Other things being equal, however, there is a preference for residing near the wife's parents' home.

Another difference between north and south Kalinga exists in the relatives who aid and contribute labor in the construction of a house for a newly married couple. In cases of uxorilocal residence in Lubuagan, only the bride's relatives are responsible for providing labor and costs, but in Mabaca and the northern Kalinga area generally, the responsibility is binding on both the bride's and groom's relatives. This difference is undoubtedly due to the fact that Mabaca, like other sparsely populated northern Kalinga regions, considers itself a single kinship unit and all its members believe themselves related.

One important point needs clarification. When informants speak of the responsibility of relatives in small group tasks such as housebuilding, they actually mean the closest kin, hence siblings, parents, parental aunts and uncles, and perhaps first cousins and the spouses of some of these. Obviously a whole kindred never engages in group work.

Members of an extended household work together in common economic tasks. In the rice fields and swiddens both sexes help, though certain jobs are more specifically for men and others for women. Only men, for example, plow, while women characteristically attend to weeding. The transportation of loads from field to house is also usually done by the women, but men may use the balance-pole for carrying heavy loads. Around the house the women help one another in pounding and winnowing rice and attend to a myriad of other tasks. Except for housebuilding and house repair, men do not have as much to do around the house as women. Characteristically in a Kalinga home, one sees men and boys sitting or lounging around while women and girls are busy with household tasks. The Kalinga women are not subdued or abused and probably have a more equal position with men than the women of other Mountain Province peoples; nevertheless, on many occasions, women will be working while men are merely around, watching and talking. This may be a phenomenon reflecting the past, when men of the household had to be free and ready to defend the home against an enemy attack.

While the extended family works together and the products of the field are shared, a single-dwelling house is ordinarily the domain of the nuclear family; occasionally a dependent relative and, in the north, a married daughter or son and her or his children, may also reside there. In the house, the couple construct special shelves along the walls to display their Chinese plates and jars which they have inherited from their parents. In a wooden closet or in a chest are other heirlooms, agate beads strung in necklaces and chokers, and brass gongs, plus woven blankets and clothes for wife, husband and the children. These are the prized possessions of the family and determine its wealth and, hence, are one index of prestige in the hamlet or region. The nuclear family also prepares meals and eats as a unit, but when visitors are entertained or on festive occasions (see Chapter 2), other relatives will be accommodated within the house to partake of a meal. There is, of course, considerable daily visiting and members of the extended household freely enter one another's houses.

Young children sleep with their parents, while unmarried children above the age of six sleep together in different houses of the extended family unit, one night in one house, the next in another, and so on. In Lubuagan unmarried youths often sleep in vacant houses called *obog* (sleeping mat), and girls in the homes of widows. Lubuagan informants also report that unmarried youths may visit girls staying in the homes of widows, or even visit girls in their homes at night, but only engaged couples are permitted to remain the night together and have sexual intercourse. Northern Kalinga patterns vary from those of Lubuagan. Here, a boy and a girl may arrange to have sexual intercourse, but this is always done secretly and not with parental approval. If a girl is forced into the act, the boy's relatives are assessed fines. If the girl is discovered, especially if she becomes pregnant, her parents will whip her provided that she entered into the affair willingly. There is no punishment of the boy if the girl consented, except to try to force him to marry her—an affair of the regional leaders (*pangats*). In the northern Kalinga area, unmarried youths and girls who are "properly raised" remain in the homes of the extended household at night and only an engaged couple may sleep together after a gift of beads following the performance of the ceremony called *ingilin*. (For further details on the subject of courting and marriage, see Chapter 2.)

It is difficult to locate the nucleus of authority in group tasks involving the extended household since direction and discipline, whether of children or adults, appear to be unstructured. Yet things get done and activity is not haphazard but orderly. Extended household decisions and work projects emanate from the older relatives, particularly the senior couple, but orders are so subtle that the extended family appears to act by precept rather than by a perceptible familial authority system.

The extended household is a kind of a segment of the larger kinship circle described below. While an older couple's daughters and their families live nearby, their married sons are dispersed in the residential areas of their respective wives' closest kin. Nevertheless, the families of sons and daughters plus a host of other relatives are members of the same kinship circle, as we shall see.

The Kinship Circle or Kindred and the Bilateral Descent Group

The important social unit of the Kalinga is a bilateral grouping of kin consisting for any individual of his siblings, first cousins, second cousins, third cousins, and the ascendants and descendants of these up through the great-grandparents and down through the great-grandchildren on both the paternal and maternal sides. Barton (1949) designated this unit the "kinship circle" while Eggan (1960) refers to it as a "personal kindred." This grouping is found among all the mountain peoples of northern Luzon. It is important to note that as the Kalinga conceive of it, this kinship unit includes the spouses of the kin named above. The terms kinship circle and personal kindred are used in this report for this grouping.

In addition to the Kalinga-type kinship circles, other Mountain Province peoples are reported to have bilateral descent groups (Eggan 1960; Lambrecht 1953, 1954). These are quasi-corporate groups consisting of the descendants of certain prominent ancestors, founding fathers, and important, living individuals. Bilateral descent groups of the Mountain Province are similar to prominent family groups in the United States like the Du Ponts, the Rockefellers, and others. One may enjoy the prestige and often the wealth of belonging to such families whether the linkage is through one's mother or father. Bilateral descent group affiliation is unlike membership in unilineal organizations like a clan, where affiliation through one parent only is strictly prescribed. The resulting structure of a bilateral descent group is a pyramid, at the apex of which stands the prominent ancestor. Some bilateral descent groups like those of the Ifugao go back many generations into the past; others have fairly shallow depths historically. Bilateral descent groups often have functional parallels with unilineal organizations. Mountain Province bilateral descent groups, for example, pass on statuses and in some cases control water rights and manage the planting and harvesting of rice. Unlike unilineal organizations, however, bilateral descent groups do not form continuing discrete units, for as new prestigeful individuals emerge, such individuals become the foci of new bilateral descent groups.

The bilateral descent group is quite a different kind of organization from the personal kindred. While in bilateral descent groups the whole group receives emphasis, in personal kindreds the individual is the focus of attention. In the personal kindred every individual is a hub in an enormous wheel of relatives spiraling outward and bounded in the outer perimeters by great-grandparents, third cousins, and great-grandchildren. As will be noted in the foregoing pages, the personal kindred among the Kalinga is important primarily with respect to the blood-feud system. (For more detailed information on kinship units of these types see Goodenough 1955; Davenport 1959.)

With the exception of three heads of families responsible for areas of irrigated rice fields in Lubuagan (south Kalinga), I found no evidence of bilateral descent groups among the Kalinga. Lubuagan rice fields are said to be divided into an upper, middle, and lower field and each of these has a supervisor who, in the past at least, was responsible for allocating water rights, announcing the times for planting and harvesting, and in settling disputes over land in his respective area.

No hint of descent groups was found among the Northern Kalinga except in connection with the recent peace pact. Positions of leadership or prominence in a region in the northern Kalinga area are acquired by individuals through individual achievement, not because they belong to specific families. There are no positions which descend along fmily lines, and while certain families are considered to be more wealthy than others, there is no ranking of common and prominent families. Nor are fields or property held in common by specific families. Inheritance patterns run along individual lines rather than along family lines.

Where there is some evidence of bilateral descent groups among the Kalinga, they are associated with rice fields and irrigation and in Lubuagan where the population density is highest. In the north, where populations are small and settlements dispersed, there is no evidence of descent groups. I did not have an opportunity to check the presence or absence of bilateral families in the Tinglayan municipal district, but informants report greater attention devoted to agriculture in Bangad with head men responsible for enforcing "no trespassing" prohibitions and other taboos in rice fields and granaries during planting and harvesting.

It seems, therefore, that bilateral descent groups in the Mountain Province occur with peoples among whom the wet-rice complex is deeply entrenched, where patterns of the ownership and inheritance of rice fields are well established, population densities high, and the rules governing the control and allocation of water rights well defined. Wealth differentials, which are particularly emphasized in the south, is an additional factor which favors the singling out of certain families for special attention. In the north, authority is informal and changing to the degree that the leader or leaders hold the respect of the shifting swidden farmers. In the past, the situation may have been like a band organization with band chiefs who acquired their positions informally and held them as long as they were responsible and respected leaders. To the extent that populations remained small and the boundaries of the region were specified and well defined, the kinship circle or kindred, with its strong informal leaders, functioned effectively. Elsewhere, for example among the Maori and in Tikopia, the bilateral descent group is associated with societies more complex than the Kalinga. In these societies factors of wealth and rank are closely associated and hence, descent from distinguished ancestors of wealth and rank are important. In Lubuagan, the term *kadangyan* refers to a well-to-do and distinguished class but its members are not deeply rooted in the society and the *pangats,* informal but influential leaders, come from all ranks. In the north there is not even an incipient development of the *kadangyan.* A well-to-do individual or family is called *bagnang,* as indeed is also the case in Lubuagan and the Kalinga generally. The important point to be noted is that in the south there is recognition of an emerging aristocratic class which is not yet firmly established, while there is not even such awareness in the north. Among the Northern Kalinga, leaders were those who had a distinguished headhunting record and who, in addition, spoke with courage and conviction at public gatherings. With the cessation of headhunting, wealth has become an important criterion of leadership, but the ability to speak with eloquence at meetings is still an important trait of the regional leader among both the Northern and Southern Kalinga.

Members of a kinship circle everywhere among the Kalinga are required to support one another in all disputes and conflicts. They are obligated to avenge any member who is killed, wounded, or wronged in any manner. They are responsible to see that the provisions of a peace pact are kept, and if any member has wronged a member of another kinship circle, all members of the kinship circle are required to contribute in the payment of indemnities. The relatives who compose the kinship circle are evident particularly on occasions such as sickness rites or funerals. At these times, specific relatives have certain obligations regarding the contribution of wine or food and receive shares of meat.

Barton (1949:32) found in Lubuagan that the kinship circle of any individual consisted of "his brothers and sisters, first cousins, second cousins, third cousins, and of the ascendants and descendants of all these categories with the exception of the descendants of the last one." Thus, above ego's generation the grandparents and their siblings are included, but below, the descendants of the third cousins are excluded altogether. In my later investigations in Lubuagan, informants drew the limits even more narrowly around the outer boundaries of the grandparental siblings, second cousins and their grandchildren. This further change very probably reflects modern acculturative pressures already evident during the time of Barton's study, when the descendants of the third cousins had been excluded from the kinship circle. Since the war there has been greater mobility and members of a kinship circle are no longer in constant face-to-face interaction as in the past. Moreover, the large populations of southern Kalinga regions make it difficult to draw the limits of the kinship circle around more distantly related kin than second cousins. The kinship circle thus appears to have shrunk in size under the pressure of acculturation and population increase.

The acculturative factors which have apparently reduced the kinship circle or kindred of the Lubuagan Kalinga are also operative in the north, but the population increase has not been as phenomenal. None of the northern regions have the high population density of the Lubuagan region and undoubtedly this factor is crucial in accounting for the reduction of the kinship circle in Lubuagan. The Northern Kalinga are still characterized by the larger kinship circle as initially described and indeed equate the territorial region with the kinship circle.

As we have noted, formerly the region was an autonomous political unit insofar as the natives conceive of the region as comprising a kinship group. In actuality, of course, members of a region do not comprise a single kinship circle but because members usually marry within the region, they tend to be closely related. With increasing marriages outside the group, at present it would be safe to predict that in the future the region will diminish in importance as the modern municipal district begins to fulfill the needs of local government. The kinship circle, perhaps in diminished size as at Lubuagan, will undoubtedly persist in importance for settling disputes. Since so many social, economic, and religious functions are bound up in the kinship circle, the continuity of this organization is virtually assured. Indeed, despite strong acculturation pressures, this kinship group has persisted in other areas of the Philippines.

In all Kalinga areas marriage to kin is strictly forbidden through first cousins. There is some objection to marrying second cousins, which occasionally occurs, while marriage with third cousins and beyond is freely condoned.

Northern and Southern Kalinga informants report that formerly regional endogamy (that is, marriage within the region) was strictly enforced. Marriages outside the region are beginning to occur, but the instances are not yet numerous. In southern Kalinga, Barton (1949:37) found two Lubuagan men married in Tanglag, the region most accessible to Lubuagan, and an informant told him about another case of a Lubuagan man who married a woman in Bangad and was living there. Barton found only one case of a woman from another region who had married into Lubuagan and resided there with her husband. The woman was also from Tanglag. A genealogy of one man's kinship circle which I collected in Lubuagan involved thirty-one married couples. Of these, five had married in from outside. The cases involved four women and one man, all residing in Lubuagan, and they had all come from regions bordering the Lubuagan region. In Mabaca, a similar genealogy of thirty-six married couples revealed only two marriages outside the region—a man married to a Balbalasan woman and another man married to a Tinguian woman from Abra. The couples were all residing in Mabaca. Marriages with Christian lowlanders are even fewer. A man from Mabongtot had formerly been married to a Tagalog woman in Manila and lived there; when she died, he married a girl from Mabilong (a town of Lubuagan), and is now residing in Mabilong. The present justice of the peace at Lubuagan, a Kalinga from Lubuagan, is married to an Ilocano woman. In Salegseg, an Ilocano teacher at the public elementary school has a Kalinga wife. Marriages between members of a parent region and colonies founded by the original region are not reckoned as marriages outside the region even though such settlements may be at considerable distance from the parent region. Marriages between parent regions and daughter settlements are the rule even after the daughter colony has gained political independence from the parent region.

The Kinship System

The kinship system is patterned on the kinship circle and singles out those relatives who are embraced in the latter. It is organized bilaterally and generationally; the terms, behavior, and obligations toward relatives extend outward from ego and his siblings. The terminology employed is similar to the American system and fits into the Eskimo type set up by Spier (1925) and Murdock (1949). Thus, cross and parallel cousins are designated by the same terms, but those used for siblings are different and never extended to cousins.*

KEY FEATURES OF THE TERMINOLOGY   Some interesting differences between the Northern Kalinga and the Lubuagan Kalinga appear in the terms employed. These differences undoubtedly reflect social and cultural changes going on in the two areas. Thus, for example, the Kalinga of the Lubuagan region use the same referential term, *olitog*, for parents' male and female siblings and the first and second cousins of parents (and spouses of all these relatives). The Northern Kalinga use *olitog* for uncles, but they have a separate term, *ikit*, for aunts and parents' female cousins through the second cousins (including wives of these relatives). The use of a single term for one's uncles and aunts is unusual in the Philippines and apparently does not exist among other Mountain Province peoples. Since the areas in which this pattern occurs were the most isolated before the American period, this usage may be the earlier Kalinga pattern. No obvious behavioral correlates have been noted with these differences in terminology between the two areas.

Another important difference in terminological usage between the two Kalinga areas is that the Northern Kalinga extend the terms of address for mother, *ina*, and father, *ama*, to parents' siblings, but the Kalinga of the Lubuagan region do not do this. Lubuagan Kalinga use personal names in addressing these relatives, as they do also for other relatives where the Northern Kalinga employ kinship terms, for example, ego's first and second cousins. It seems possible to explain these changes by the rather phenomenal population increase in the Lubuagan region, an explanation which we have also suggested for the reduction of the Lubuagan kinship circle. Lubuagan Kalinga recognize that the use of personal names for relatives is a recent change. "We are too proud and are beginning to lose respect for our relatives," they remarked when I asked why they did not employ relationship terms as do their northern kin. Interaction in Lubuagan is depersonalized and even close relatives do not interact with the intimacy and closeness that characterize interpersonal relations in the north. Lubuagan has an urban aspect with some of the same impersonalized and individualized traits that characterize urban settlements elsewhere.

Among the Kalinga generally, the nuclear or elementary family is not set apart as distinctly as elsewhere in the Mountain Province (Eggan 1960:38). While collective terms such as "father and child" and "mother and child" exist, these are no more frequently employed than terms like "grandparent and child." Further, parent terms are not as widely extended. The greater importance of the extended household also tends to deemphasize the nuclear family. Thus, among the Kalinga, a wider circle of kin appears to receive greater attention in the terminology and in the behavior of relatives. This kin group is the personal kindred or kinship circle,

---

* See Schusky (1965) for useful explanations, designed for the instruction of beginning students, of different types of kinship systems.

whether the wider one of Northern Kalinga or the narrower one of the Lubuagan Kalinga.

KINSHIP BEHAVIOR   Obligations and responsibilities among kin are particularly emphasized on ceremonial occasions associated with the life cycle and in the operation of inheritance patterns. The life cycle will be discussed in greater detail in a special section; here I will record the generalized behavior among relatives that occurs during the round of ordinary daily life. It has been noted that the Lubuagan Kalinga tend to address relatives by the use of personal names rather than by the use of kin terms. The Northern Kalinga use kin terms in address to a greater extent than the Southern Kalinga, but compared to the Kankanay of Sagada (Eggan 1960) the Kalinga tend to use kin terms less extensively in address. As already suggested, this phenomenon may reflect acculturative factors which have influenced the kinship circle in special ways. Intimate interpersonal relations among kin have been disrupted in Lubuagan by increased population; but the high mobility of the Kalinga everywhere has also modified the intimate face-to-face interaction among relatives which we believe to have characterized the regions formerly.

GRANDPARENT-GRANDCHILDREN   Children develop a feeling of extreme fondness for their grandparents. This is because so many of the early years of a child's life are spent in the company of a grandfather or grandmother. With the predominantly uxorilocal pattern of residence, the grandparents a child sees most often are the maternal ones, although this is not an invariable rule. There is so much visiting of kin in the region that even if one's grandchildren are not near, there are frequent occasions when contact with grandchildren occurs. Then, as noted, not all married couples establish matrilocal or uxorilocal residence; a few in each barrio or *sitio* live near the husband's parents' home or, in the case of the Northern Kalinga, the couple may establish residence in a settlement where neither pair of parents resides.

Grandparents are the baby-sitters of the Kalinga. While the parents are working in the fields, the young children are left in the care of a grandfather or grandmother or both. Children are delighted to be with grandparents since the latter are more indulgent than their parents. If a grandfather is still strong and active he will transport his grandchild about the village in a blanket sling and permit the child to see a variety of daily activities. Grandmothers restrict themselves more closely to the home with their charges, but both shower their grandchildren with affectionate attention.

A child is often given the name of a living or departed grandparent. The Kalinga believe that conferring the name of a person on a child magically transfers the attributes of its namesake, whether of longevity, prominence, or any other desired quality. Related to this belief is the one that if a grandchild dies within a few months after the death of a grandparent, the spirit of the latter has taken the grandchild. The grandparent who has been especially affectionate to a grandchild is believed to be a kind of guardian spirit to the child after the former's death. Hence, a grandchild must be especially attentive to grandparents and fulfill all obligations entailed in the relationship.

Grandchildren have the responsibility of seeing that grandparents are well cared for in their old age. While ordinarily they do not inherit directly from the grandparents, they are, nevertheless, obligated to offer sacrifices at the time of a grandparent's illness or at his or her funeral. In Lubuagan during a curing rite for a grandparent, the grandchildren join in singing the funeral songs (*mangbikbik*). Also in Lubuagan at the grandparent's funeral, grandchildren play conventionalized games and run races, with prizes being awarded the winners. Thus, as small children they are involved in ceremonies given for a grandparent. Later, as adults, grandchildren initiate or take a prominent part in illness and funeral ceremonies for their grandparents.

When a person is ill, the medium (*manalisig,* Lubuagan; *mandadawak, mananito,* Northern Kalinga) often prescribes sacrifices to be made to a dead grandparent after having "discovered" that the spirit of a departed grandparent has been offended or not properly propitiated. Most illnesses among the Kalinga are believed to be caused by dead ancestors who make known their wants by sending illness or misfortune. If a medium names a grandparent as the cause of an illness, the patient and his relatives have a curing rite and the animals butchered on the occasion are offered to the spirit of the deceased grandparent.

A mild form of joking exists between a grandparent and a grandchild. The former teases the grandchild about lack of work aptitudes, failure to secure a sweetheart or wife, or flaws in the partner he or she has been contracted to marry. In turn, the grandchild chides the grandparent about infirmities and inability to do a full day's work. But this is all in fun and the relationship between a grandfather and grandson and a grandmother and granddaughter is undoubtedly the most affectionate bond in Kalinga society.

Much of Kalinga culture, particularly with respect to ceremonial practices and beliefs, is learned from grandparents. A grandparent often selects a specific grandchild upon whom to devote special emotional attention and affection. In such cases, a strong bond of affection and dependence is forged, lasting until the death of one or the other. Such a bond existed between one of my informants from the region of Poswoy (northern Kalinga) and his maternal grandfather. His death recently was such a blow that the death of any other member of his family would not have been so keenly felt. My informant slept with his grandfather under the same blanket until late in his youth, and accompanied the former in travels in many parts of northern Kalinga. The grandfather encouraged him to continue his education, even though other members of the family wanted him to come home and take up farming. It is the advice and counsel of this grandfather that he now cherishes and hopes to follow in life.

PARENT-CHILD RELATIONSHIP   Between the ages of about two and six, children are usually left in the care of grandparents or older siblings. Mothers are busy with younger siblings or else are performing essential household tasks and helping in the rice fields. Weaning takes place at any time between the ages of one and five, depending on whether or not younger siblings have put in an appearance in the family. If there are no younger siblings, a child may nurse until the age of five. Such a child sees a great deal of its mother and develops close ties with her, but if there are many children, only the youngest may get special attention.

In Lubuagan, after the age of about six or seven, girls sleep together with agemates in the homes of widows, while boys go to an *obog,* a vacant house habitually used as a sleeping place. Thus, parents in Lubuagan become even more separated from their children after these ages. There is, of course, considerable interaction with children during the day and contact continues with those children, especially daughters, who bring their spouses to reside near the parental home. Nevertheless, parent-child relationships are not as intense and prolonged among the Kalinga as among other groups.

The Northern Kalinga do not segregate the children in the Lubuagan manner. Parents in the north maintain closer and more prolonged contact with their children. Thus, children ordinarily remain with their families until the time they join or are joined by their contracted partner before marriage and a separate dwelling is erected for them. After this, interaction continues in extended household living or in the custom of frequent visiting.

Fathers in the evenings devote considerable time to children, playing with the young ones, carrying infants in blanket slings. Later the boys accompany their fathers to the fields, while girls remain at home to care for younger siblings, although some will also work in the fields. Boys bring fuel, but their help and duties around the house are considerably less than the tasks required of and performed by their sisters.

Parents seldom resort to whipping, but scold or frighten children into obedience. Strangers often become bogy men and children may be told that strangers will carry them away if they do not behave. Lubuagan and Northern Kalinga informants reported spanking children in severe cases of disobedience, but this is rare and I personally did not observe it. Kalinga child-rearing practices may be characterized as indulgent and permissive. The Northern Kalinga will whip an adolescent girl who has sex relations with a man not contracted to her in marriage, with a man already married, or with one who has not promised to marry the girl. The boy or the man escapes punishment, unless he has forced the girl into the relationship; in the latter case, he must pay heavy fines. The Kalinga are motivated in these matters not by moral or ethical principles but by practical concerns. Support and inheritance are crucial matters and when these are complicated or threatened, parents and relatives take action to see that sons and daughters are insured economic support and their inheritance protected. Marriages are arranged for this reason and while an engaged couple may break their contract, parents make every effort to hold together a couple whose contract is considered a sound economic arrangement. By safeguarding the inheritance due a son and daughter and by providing a good match, economically viewed, parents feel that they have fulfilled their primary obligation to their children. Moreover, they have also guaranteed their own future in this life and the next. Children are obligated to provide for the economic support of their parents when the latter became old or infirm, to offer the proper sacrifices when thay are sick and again at their funerals, and to continue to make such sacrifices for their well-being in the hereafter.

The Kalinga are a practical people and the concern over their children is practical and realistic. Whereas parent-child relations are not completely devoid of affection, they contrast sharply with the warmth and love that a grandparent showers on a grandchild. The latter relationship is not ordinarily a bond of mutual obligations. The grandparent has already given out his inheritance to his own sons and daughters who have the primary obligations for reciprocal payments in the form of economic support and sacrifices to the spirit on the behalf of the grandparent after his death.

UNCLES AND AUNTS, NEPHEWS AND NIECES   Aunts and uncles assume the status and responsibility of parents in the absence of the latter. If a child is orphaned, an aunt or uncle takes the child into his household. Here, the child becomes like another member of the family and his rights of inheritance are equal to those of the other children. The child also has equal obligation with his first cousins to support his foster parents in their old age and to offer sacrifices in their behalf. The behavior of an adopted niece or nephew is said not to differ in any respect from that of the other children. Indeed, it is believed that adopted children are often more attentive to aged foster parents than real children and that they are more careful in offering sacrifices at times of illness and at the death of their foster parents.

The Northern Kalinga appear to have closer relations with their aunts and uncles than in Lubuagan. We have noted the extension of parent terms in address to uncles and aunts among the former, but not at Lubuagan where the personal names of these relatives are used. There is also more sharing of cooperative activities, such as house building, the construction of swiddens and the like, with these relatives and ego's household. Undoubtedly this is due to the smaller populations in the north where kinship relations are known and kept tab on more closely than in the south. Among both the north and south Kalinga, an adopted nephew or niece employs sibling terms for his or her aunt's or uncle's children with whom he resides, but sibling terms are not otherwise extended to cousins.

Often an influential uncle becomes a kind of father confessor and counselor to his sister's or brother's family. When this family is in difficulty, it may consult the uncle who is always ready to offer sage advice and to preform many kinds of services for them. One of my companions and aides, a young man of about twenty-five who drew maps for me, counted houses in hamlets and performed a number of other useful tasks, could not bring himself to tell me that he was needed at home and could no longer work for me. He walked from his own village to an isolated hamlet where an uncle lived and brought him over the next day so that the uncle could tell me that his nephew could no longer work for me! This incident also illustrates another interesting trait of the Kalinga. They cannot divulge unpleasant news directly but must bring a relative along, most often an uncle, to explain the circumstances.

The homes of uncles and aunts are constant visiting places for nephews and nieces. Most traveling within a region is to visit relatives and these are usually uncles and aunts. If a child is scolded or reprimanded in any way, he or she will take the first opportunity to visit an uncle or aunt, often traveling several miles to discuss the incident. Frequently he will return with the aunt or uncle to talk over the matter with his parents, the uncle or aunt attempting to smooth over the difficulty.

SIBLINGS AND COUSINS   Ego and his siblings, ego's first cousins, the latter's parents and ego's own parents form a circle of kin where obligations and privileges are most clearly defined. This is the group of relatives among whom intermarriage is strictly prohibited, even with former spouses of the group who have been widowed or divorced. These relatives support one another in all disputes and troubles and also rejoice together in any good fortune that befalls one of their members or the group as a whole. Respectful behavior marks the relationship among all these relatives.

Beyond first cousins, laterally, obligations and privileges extend to second cousins in Lubuagan and among the Northern Kalinga to third cousins. In the north where kinship group and region are believed to be coextensive, obligations and privileges of the kinship circle are extended to all members of the regional population. If a regional member is killed, wounded or injured in any manner by someone from the outside, all those living in the region are obligated to avenge since they are all considered relatives and very likely can trace relationships to at least the third cousin degree. If an offense is committed among members of the region, the matter is taken up by the influential leaders of the region who discuss the matter and decide on fines and payments to be made. Since all consider themselves relatives, vengeance is seldom resorted to in intraregional disputes. While injuries are often inflicted by hotheaded individuals in a quarrel within a region, influential leaders are ready to separate such individuals. Heated arguments are casually stopped before they go very far by emphasizing that everyone is related and must support one another.

In the densely populated Lubuagan region, kinship allegiances and responsibilities have become complicated and confused beyond the first cousin degree of relationship. While kinfolk within the second cousin degree of relationship (the lateral boundaries of the kinship circle) are all required to support one another, increased populations have disrupted face-to-face relations and one is not always sure which relatives he is supposed to defend or avenge. This is particularly so since second cousins may marry; therefore, in disputes involving individuals related to both parties, it is not always possible to know whether one should take vengeance, pay indemnities, take precautions not to be avenged upon, or to collect indemnities. The result is considerable feuding and fighting and even occasional killings within the region (Barton 1949:69–83). The important difference between Lubuagan and the northern Kalinga regions is that in the former region the vengeance pattern is frequently invoked, whereas in the north vengeance tends to operate only interregionally, and intravillage disputes are informally resolved by amicable settlements.

AFFINAL OR IN-LAW RELATIONS   All spouses married to consanguineal relatives (that is, those related by blood) of the kinship circle are also members of the group and theoretically at least, have the same responsibilities and privileges. Again, it is important to note that, as in the case of relatives more distant than first cousins, spouses have divided loyalties and obligations to their own consanguineal kin; thus, their cooperation is complicated in the Lubuagan region and in the south Kalinga regions where kinship group and region are not considered to be coextensive. The endogamous regions of the north work as a unit and spouses are part of this relationship.

The sibling terms are used when speaking to men and women married to ego's siblings. These relatives are treated in a respectful manner and they are not avoided. As elsewhere in the Mountain Province (Eggan 1960:38), children are essential for a stable and enduring marriage. If no children result from a union, separation or divorce is customary and the gifts exchanged are returned or some settlement agreeable to both families is made. Each partner may then contract another marriage with the hope that the new relationship will produce children.

Parents-in-law are treated with respect and obedience much in the same manner as real parents, but they are not addressed by parent terms. A marriage unites the parents of the couple in a special relationship and henceforth they become *abalan*, co-parents-in-law, to one another. While the son-in-law or daughter-in-law treats his or her parent-in-law with respect and obedience, there are no avoidance or restrictive patterns between them.

Because of the uxorilocal character of Kalinga extended households, it is the men who most often change residence to live in the proximity of their in-laws. Thus, the man ordinarily makes the greatest adjustments after marriage with respect to relationships with in-laws. The inability to get along with in-laws may sometimes lead to separation and divorce, but this is rare. The overwhelming cause for divorce is attributed to the lack of children. In the south Kalinga area, kinship feuds within the region were also given as a cause for divorce, but there are many cases where a man and woman remained married despite family disputes.

The kinship system of the Kalinga is involved almost solely with consanguineal and affinal relatives. Except in connection with the peace pact institution, which is a recent development, there is no evidence of an indigenous ritual kinship organization. The trading partnership, *aboyog*, bound two individuals from different regions into a pact of mutual obligations of hospitality and physical protection for one another and their companions, but such relationships were usually short lived. Moreover, neither the two individuals nor their families were bound into a blood-brother relationship, as they are elsewhere in the Philippines and in Southeast Asia. There was also no extension of kinship terms to one another or their families and no behavior that would suggest even remotely a feeling of kinship between the relatives of the two individuals bound in an *aboyog* relationship. The development of the Kalinga peace pact institution has essentially replaced the trading partnership, and trade, visiting, and other interregional contacts now go on under the protection and privileges extended by the peace pact. Between peace pact holders of two different regions and their families some aspects of the kinship system have been extended. There is no ritual to make pact-holders "brothers" but they are considered as such, and marriage prohibitions are binding on their relatives just as if they were all members of the same kinship circle. Obligations that are traditional to members of a kinship circle such as attendance and assistance at marriages, funerals, and the like are also extended. Distances between regions and difficulties of travel, however, make it impossible for pact-holders and members of their kinship group to fulfill, even minimally, such obligations. There is also no extension of kinship terms, even among the two pact holders themselves. A peace pact is intended to open up intermarriage privileges between members of the two regions (except for the pact-holders and their families), but traditional vengeance and inheritance patterns conflict with such practices and mixed marriages are placed in a difficult position.

The godparent system known in Latin America as *compadrazgo* (Mintz and Wolf 1950), introduced among lowland Filipinos by the early Spanish missionaries and now an important institution among them, has had little effect on the Kalinga. Occasionally a Kalinga will exchange *compadre* and *comadre* terms with Ilocano baptismal or marriage sponsors (his own or those of his children), but the obligations inherent in the system are either unknown or ignored. Blood ties, reckoned bilaterally, thus form the basis of Kalinga social and regional unity.

2

From Birth to Death

FOUR STAGES in the life cycle of an individual are given social and ceremonial significance among the Kalinga: birth, marriage, sickness, and death. There is considerable variation in the manner in which these ceremonies are conducted in the different regions and some life-cycle events recognized in one region may not be presented in another. Yet there is a similar pattern of Kalinga life-cycle observances despite regional variations. The following account is from the regions of Poswoy and Mabaca (northern Kalinga) with some comparative comments about practices in the Lubuagan region (southern Kalinga).

Pregnancy and Birth

Children are greatly desired among the Kalinga and though large numbers are born, many do not survive into adulthood. Sample genealogical records for the regions of Lubuagan and Mabaca indicate averages of 7 children per family over a normal child-bearing period of a woman, while the size of households are 5.5 for the Mabaca region of north Kalinga and 4.8 for the Lubuagan region of south Kalinga. There seems to be a high rate of barrenness among women, and perhaps the fertility rate of men is also low. At any rate, there are a number of marriages where no children are born. Normally in such cases the couple will separate in order to try their luck with other partners. If there are no children from an individual's second marriage, he or she will separate again. The number of divorces is high among the Kalinga; as many as 50 percent of the men presently married in the region of Poswoy have been divorced at least once. Such divorces are almost always because the woman did not conceive. A woman refuses to accept that she is barren and keeps trying to have children with different partners until the onset of menopause. In some cases a wife will permit a husband to have a mistress (*dagdagas*) with the agreement among all three that if there are any children from this arrangement, one of them will be raised as the married couple's own. In other cases, a devoted couple who do not wish to separate may adopt the child of a relative so that there is an heir to property and someone to offer sacrifices for the couple in time of illness and after death.

The inability of a woman to have a child is attributed to three possible factors among the Northern Kalinga: (1) a disregard of bad omens at the time of marriage, (2) the activity of the *ngilin,* a malevolent water spirit who is believed to have the appearance of a human pigmy, and (3) to an organic or physical defect in the reproductive organs of the woman. In the first and second instances, the couple "pretend to separate" in order to make the *ngilin* believe that the couple have given up trying to have a child. It is believed that by this action the *ngilin* will turn up its attention elsewhere and while it is distracted the couple can resume sexual relations assured that without the machinations of the *ngilin* the wife will conceive. The *ngilin* is reported to consume the spirits of human embryos or newly born children. Other spirits, particularly the ancestral spirits of grandparents, are also believed to take unborn or newly born children with them into the spirit world.

An organic or physical defect in a woman which prevents her from conceiving is diagnosed by a woman doctor by examination. Such a native doctor, of which there are a few in every region, will treat the wife and prescribe certain acts for both the wife and the husband to perform. In Poswoy there are three women who, by bathing and massaging the woman and administering herbal drinks to both husband and wife, are believed to bring about fertility in the woman. For a tilted womb, native women doctors are able to straighten the womb. This is done immediately after menses when the womb is soft and the opening into the uterus is enlarged.

Informants from Poswoy denied that there were sacrifices performed by native doctors to induce fertility. In Lubuagan, however, a medium is called to perform a ceremony (*makobin*) over a barren woman. A medium butchers a pig and sings the chants that are appropriate for the ceremony. She instructs the woman to visit her husband's parents and tells the husband to distribute gifts among his wife's relatives. Apparently the general good feeling thus generated between the two sets of relatives, wife's and husband's, is believed to bring about fertility.

Pregnancy among the Kalinga is marked by intricate ritual practices and observances of numerous restrictions by both husband and wife. These customs are observed in order to maintain the health of the mother, to facilitate easy birth, and to safeguard the health of the unborn child.

The Kalinga woman is considered to be temperamental and jealous of her husband during pregnancy. She becomes angry if her husband comes home late from the fields and is morose and sullen if her husband spends too much time with friends. She is likely to flare up with anger at her husband on the least provocation and may tear his clothes, or release her anger by spanking her children. A pregnant woman also develops a peculiar desire to special foods, such as shrimp and fruits that are difficult to obtain. A particularly typical craving of pregnant Kalinga women is for sour fruits and vegetables. The husband is said to be patient and understanding during this time and will attempt to humor her and fulfill as many of her desires as possible.

Some women are often nauseated during pregnancy and cannot retain their food. It is believed in Poswoy that this condition is caused by the husband eating foods such as beef, cow's milk, eel, frogs, *gabi* (taro), and dog meat—all of which are prohibited to a couple during the wife's pregnancy. If the woman has serious trouble in retaining food and grows thin, a medium is called to perform a ceremony called *yabyab* (see below).

During the wife's pregnancy, both husband and wife must avoid places where *ngilin,* the water spirit, might be encountered. The *ngilin* resides in streams, particularly in pools and waterfalls. It is believed that the *ngilin* is attracted by the odor of a pregnant woman and even a husband or her children may carry this odor. If the *ngilin* smells the odor, he learns of the pregnant woman and will devour her unborn child.

The following restrictions are observed during the period of pregnancy: A pregnant woman must not eat eggs for the baby may be born blind; she must not use a cup made out of taro leaves for drinking because this would cause her child to be easily dominated by others; older children must not sit by doors or windows when a baby is expected lest the baby be born in a breach position; the father must avoid playing the flute during labor because the child may become an incessant cry baby.

After birth the child is still in danger of being harmed by the *ngilin.* These fears of the *ngilin* are lost only after the removal of restrictions on visiting and food taboos following a ceremony to remove such restrictions.

While there is a desire for children and a home without children is not considered the natural state of affairs among the Kalinga, Kalinga women also feel that too many children present hardships on the mother. In the north, at least, some women who have too many children consult an abortionist. There are specially knowledgeable women who perform abortions by administering a drink prepared from an herb called *gallopot,* and with the aid of massage. In the region of Poswoy, a woman who has had eleven children, ten of them living, considered abortion for future pregnancies, but her relatives advised against it. Restricting the size of the family becomes a problem for the bilateral kin group because of inheritance customs. All children are entitled to a share in the property of parents and that of the grandparents as well if the latter's property has not been divided. The parents of a large family may claim a greater share of their own parents' property; hence, a large family poses problems not only for the nuclear family involved but for parental siblings and their children as well. Abortion is then not only a concern of a wife and her husband but of all the bilateral kin whose share of inheritance might be smaller if more children are to share in the division of property. In this particular Poswoy case, the bilateral kin advised against abortion, thereby leaving open the possibility of more children and hence more claimants to inherited property.

The Lubuagan Kalinga have a special ceremony, *manilom,* to celebrate pregnancy of a woman, offset evil consequences, and placate the spirits. When a girl realizes that she is pregnant, she informs her husband and her parents and arrangements are made to have the *manilom.* Pigs are butchered and the medium comes to sing and bless the event. The celebration is a two-day affair with a gathering of relatives from both the husband's and wife's side.

The Northern Kalinga do not appear to have anything comparable to the Lubuagan *manilom*. Poswoy has a special sickness rite, the *yabyab*, for pregnant women, but this is a curing ceremony rather than a celebration rite. Of course, the *manilom* is not simply a celebration rite either since its performance is also, or perhaps primarily, to ward off any possible ill effects on the woman and the expected child and, hence, to insure a safe and satisfactory delivery.

The Poswoy *yabyab* ceremony is performed only for a special type of illness to which pregnant women are believed to be subject. This malady causes the woman to lose weight and to become gaunt and weak. A medium is engaged who sacrifices a small pig. The heart of the pig is rubbed on the breasts and back of the woman. A feast is prepared to which all the relatives of the couple in the immediate vicinity of the sick woman's house are invited. For other types of illness suffered by a pregnant woman, or for a difficult labor, the medium performs the regular Kalinga curing rite called *dawak* (Northern Kalinga), or *posipos* (Lubuagan). The chants sung by the medium for *yabyab* differ from those of the *dawak* or *posipos*, although there appears to be considerable variation in the curing chants from region to region (see Chapter 3).

A curing rite for the married couple also exists in Poswoy. This right, *sabblay*, is specifically for husband and wife in Poswoy. If both husband and wife become ill, a medium is engaged to perform the ceremony over them. The rite involves the sacrifice of a pig and the recitation of chants appropriate to the ceremony. For an illness of husband or wife alone, the appropriate Poswoy curing ceremony is the *dawak*.

Delivery takes place within the house. When labor pains begin, the expectant mother tells her husband, who calls her mother and other relatives of the extended household. A rope is suspended from a rafter and the woman sits on the knees of her husband or another relative. She draws on the rope while the relatives take turns in kneading and pressing on her abdomen. As the baby emerges, the woman's mother receives it. She cuts the cord with a bamboo knife and washes the baby in water which has been boiled. She then wraps the baby in the soft brown bark of the *alimit* tree. After one week, the grandmother will wash the baby again, mixing the bath water with an herb prepared from the *solsolkop* tree. This tree has hard joints and it is believed that the baby's arm and leg joints will likewise become strong.

The birth of a baby among both the Northern and Southern Kalinga is attended by restrictions in the activities of the household and by the observance of food taboos. The general name for this period of restriction is *ngilin*, the same name given to the malevolent spirit which might bring harm to an unborn or newly born child. As soon as the baby is born, an adult man or woman of the household places four knotted runo shoots (*poldos*) at every corner of the house on the outside. The runo shoots indicate that the family within is under restriction, and visitors, including relatives who do not sleep in the house, are prohibited from entering it. Food restrictions for the family at this time include the following: beef, cow's milk, eel, frogs, taro, and dog meat. Most important of all, the father must not go outside the bounds of his village during the period of restrictions.

About one month after the birth of the baby, a medium is called who asks an old woman to sweep the house with the native raincoat made of palm fronds, *anaao.* Then the old woman or the medium herself removes the knotted runo shoots signifying the end of the *ngilin.* The medium pronounces the mother and child safe and instructs the household to resume its normal functioning with all restrictions removed.

After the *ngilin,* the mother resumes her usual duties around the house, but with the added task of nursing her baby. If her milk is inadequate, she finds a mother with an extra supply of milk to supplement her feeding. Finding a wet nurse presents difficulties since the Kalinga mother believes that a woman with a baby of the same age as her own should be located. She proceeds from the nearest to more distant relatives in locating a woman to nurse her baby and she usually finds one in the large numbers that compose her kinship circle. At present, some Kalinga mothers also use canned milk preparations to supplement feeding, but canned milk presents problems. It is hard to keep milk from souring and Kalinga mothers have difficulty in observing the necessary precautions needed to safeguard the use of canned milk for infants. As a result, there is considerable illness among babies whose mothers have an inadequate supply of milk.

The Kontad Ceremonies: Infancy and Early Years

In all Kalinga areas the first year-and-a-half of a child's life is filled with a series of rather complex ceremonial rituals called *kontad* (Northern Kalinga), or *kontid* (Southern Kalinga). The word *kontad* in the north Kalinga dialects means a request or supplication. The child in its first year is considered to be most vulnerable to the machinations of malevolent spirits. The Kalinga believe, therefore, that the malevolent spirits must be placated and, hence, observe the rituals religiously. The series of ceremonies is performed by mediums who know the appropriate rituals, prayers, and chants. The Kalinga refer to these mediums by a special term, *mangkokontad,* rather than the general term for medium, *mangalisig* (Southern Kalinga), or *mandadawak* (Northern Kalinga).

Kontad rituals involve characteristic Kalinga ceremonial features and practices such as the sacrifice of chickens or pigs, the singing of chants, examination of the pig's liver for omens, and in some of the stages of the *kontad,* the erection of a spirit house or platform. These aspects of Kalinga ceremonial ritual are discussed in greater detail in Chapter 3.

The baby is given a name during the period of the *kontad.* In Poswoy the medium gives a child a name from one of its ancestors. A name might be changed later if the child becomes ill. This is done to deceive the malevolent spirits who are believed to be making the child sick. The spirits, believing that their magic has worked since they do not recognize the child under the new name, will stop the machinations.

A deceased grandparent or other near relative is also believed to make a child ill in order that the child may join him in the afterworld. The *kontad* ceremonies are performed to placate both malevolent and ancestral spirits. The belief that ancestors are responsible for illness or misfortune is stronger in the south; the north emphasizes the activity of malevolent spirits as causative agents. In Poswoy, prayers by the medium are addressed to *mandodwa*—a designation said to include all benevolent spirits.

A simple ceremony for teething called *káwol* is performed in Poswoy when the child is about four months old. A woman inserts a *sangal* bead (the most valuable of the precious beads) into the mouth of the child and as she takes it out, she says: "Come front teeth, this is the bead you have been waiting for." In Lubuagan, at about the same age, the father's parents give the child a special gift, usually a bead necklace. A pig is then butchered and close relatives of the child's father and mother are invited to partake of the festivities.

The solidarity of the kinship circle bond is periodically reinforced during the first and second year of a child's life. In Lubuagan, when a child first mentions the name of a relative, a formal visit called *omoy pasibits* is made to the particular relative's home. Similar formal visits to members of the bilateral kin group at Poswoy is called *omapó*. The first time that the baby is taken to visit the father's parents is the occasion for a special celebration called *balón di babát* (Poswoy), or *mamilók* (Lubuagan). At this time, a large pig is butchered and the kinship circles of both the mother and father come together for a grand celebration. The forefront of the pig, *longos,* is taken to the wife's relatives and the carriers are given a peso or two each. The hindquarter is cut into strips and the shares, *ilang,* distributed among the father's kindred. In addition to the large pig, additional pigs, chickens, and carabaos are also butchered on this occasion, depending on the wealth of the father's relatives. Large quantities of sugar cane wine, *basi,* are also passed around and consumed. The celebration is a prestige feast and the father's relatives make every effort to make the occasion an impressive one. In the sparsely settled regions of the north, as many as one-third of the regional population might attend the affair and all will receive a share of the meat. In Lubuagan and other densely populated regions of the south, far more people come than can be given shares of meat. Since some of those who do not receive a share of meat also reckon themselves related to the father, bitter arguments occasionally occur between the near and distant kin over the determination of who is entitled or not entitled to meat shares. Sometimes these arguments flare up into spear and head axe fights and a killing may occur. Northern Kalinga festive occasions are much more peaceful, although the men get drunk and there is formalized boasting about one's accomplishments, *manyamyam, i-iyab;* or war exploits, *pokao, palpaliwat.* Festivities in the *balón di babát* start in midafternoon and go on far into the night with gong music and dancing. As the couple leave for their home, the father's family presents the child with a precious gift, the *balón.* This is usually a necklace of beads to be cherished by the child for the rest of its life. It will form a part of his heirloom collection along with valuable Chinese jars, plates, and gongs.

The constant reiteration of the kinship bond in festivities and in daily relations among members of a region is a striking feature of Kalinga society. There is continual mobility within the region and relatives visit one another and may remain overnight. This pattern of interaction, almost solely of the regional population, even though the settlements are widely dispersed, is especially characteristic of the Northern Kalinga. In the south, intimate and frequent contacts among relatives, which we believe was the pattern in the past, has diminished with increased populations. Indeed, the changes are beginning to become evident now in the north as well. Modern conditions with the development of bus travel, trade, and wage work are beginning to distrupt the close intraregional interaction of relatives.

Weaning and toilet-training are carried out in a relaxed atmosphere with no apparent fixed or rigid rules. There are no regular periods of feeding the infant; he is given the breast whenever he desires it. There is also no set time for weaning; most children continue to nurse until quite old, up to the age of four or five if the child does not have siblings. If other children come, then the mother may discourage nursing by rubbing her breasts with powdered *sili* (chili peppers). This is said to be effective with most children; with others, shaming is believed to work. Thus, the mother works on the pride of the child by telling it that he is too old to nurse, or by comparing the child adversely to younger children in the village who have been weaned. Early, the infant is given solid food such as rice, bananas, and sweet potatoes, and is allowed to suck sugar cane. The process of weaning is, therefore, accomplished with minimal effort and Kalinga mothers do not consider it a serious problem.

Toilet-training is also treated in a similarly relaxed fashion. Bark cloth, made especially soft by careful pounding, was formerly used as diapers and today cotton cloth is sometimes employed. Most often, however, infants and toddlers are completely without clothes. Indeed, clothing does not appear on the child until he is seven or eight years old, and then it is usually a simple shirt or dress. Little attention is paid to the toddler who relieves himself on the floor of the house. If an older member of the household catches the child in time, he is quickly picked up and held over a portion of the floor where the bamboo mat floor can be lifted. Outside, the small child may relieve himself or defecate anywhere. Pigs and dogs, who roam freely about the village, quickly clean up the refuse. Indeed, pigs follow naked children around and are quick to clean up if a child has a bowel movement.

For older children, parents advise them to go to the edge of the village. Outside privies are a recent introduction and most villages still do not have these facilities. Bed-wetting problems are handled in much the same way as weaning, by shaming. In general, toilet training is accomplished without prescribed rules, simply by permitting the child to follow his own inclinations until such a time as he can understand the behavior of older children and adults in his village. Thus, the child adjusts his toilet practices to the group in order to prevent censure and ridicule.

In addition to the *kontad* series of ceremonies performed for health and well-being of the child, a ceremony called *gabbok* is performed in different regions of northern and southern Kalinga. In Lubuagan, the ceremony is considered a thanksgiving celebration and is performed three or four months after the birth of the child. A medium chants the appropriate songs associated with the ceremony. Chickens and pigs are sacrificed and relatives and friends come to join the parents in celebration.

In Poswoy, a *gabbok* is a curing rite which takes place only if the child becomes ill after the series of *kontad* ceremonies have been completed. A mature pig is sacrificed by the medium and special chants different from those of the *kontad* or the general curing rite, *dawak,* are sung.

Dawak is the general curing ceremony for the Northern Kalinga, while its counterpart in south Kalinga is called *posipos.* Upon completion of the *kontad* series and the intermediate *gabbok* rites, any subsequent illness or misfortune suffered by the child entails the performance of this general ceremony.

Later Childhood

Children are brought up in a seemingly unstructured and permissive atmosphere. Up to the age of six or seven few restrictions are placed on them, and with boys this permissive pattern is carried on considerably longer. The activities of boys and girls during the first three to four years is undifferentiated. As infants, they are carried about in blanket slings by older sisters or aged grandparents. Indeed, until an infant is able to crawl, it is rarely put down. The belief is strong that an unattended baby's spirit will be carried off by malevolent or ancestral spirits. Hence, an older sibling or adult is always around an infant. At night, the baby sleeps next to the mother, usually between the parents. From ages three to six, children may occasionally accompany their parents to the fields, but children most commonly remain in the village. Undoubtedly this is a practice from former times when the enemy was likely to attack those away from settled areas. Men and women in the prime of life can defend themselves or run back to the safety of the village, but old people and children are not so nimble; hence, they remained in the greater security of the hamlet or village.

There is no marked preference for boys or girls in the society. Since the residence pattern is predominantly uxorilocal and since women do most of the work around the house and fields, one might expect that girls would be favored; but past conditions when enemy attacks were common still dominate Kalinga thinking. Men did all the fighting and distinguished war records determined the influence and prestige of families. It was therefore important to have sons, and a family without sons was considered very unfortunate. The custom of placing few restrictions on the activity of males in the family is a reflection of conditions in earlier days when the males of the family defended homes and youths brought back heads from the enemy. Girls at an early age assume heavy household tasks and responsibilities. They care for younger siblings, pound and winnow rice, scrub the bamboo floor mats, tote water, and help in the fields. Young boys are responsible only for bringing fuel; the rest of the time they loll around whiling away time in idle gossip. For those youths who have been promised in marriage, activities are more circumscribed. They take up residence in their future wife's household and perform various services for the family. But even these youths have it far easier than girls of comparable age.

Discipline as such is not disapproved of by Kalinga. They believe, however,

that discipline should be dispensed by individuals with the authority and qualifications to do so. Parents are not considered to have these prerogatives over their
own children. Parents believe that their function is mainly to provide love and
affection. While they may suggest or shame their children into proper behavior,
serious disciplinary problems are taken to an uncle or an influential man of authority. At present, school teachers and outsiders who employ Kalinga are also
granted the right to exercise discipline. Thus, school teachers and non-Kalinga in
authoritative positions are often asked by parents to be firm and strict with their
children and to spank them "if they need it."

Serious parents deplore the idle behavior of their young sons at present, but
they seem at a loss for solutions. The freedom which boys have is, of course, a
carry-over from earlier days when, as youths and young men, they had to be free
and unencumereed to protect women, children, and the aged from enemy attacks
and on occasion to bring back heads for the glory of their families. Boys early developed a pride in warfare activities. They practiced under the supervision of older
males and soon became proficient in the use of the spear, shield, and headaxe. But
warfare is an activity of past generations; idleness today can and does lead to trouble. Young boys having no concrete and purposeful tasks to do often break into
houses to steal or vandalize; with increasing frequency, young boys become involved in arguments and disputes with relatives. Kalinga parents are ineffectual in
providing guidance and in controlling the deviant behavior of their children.

Corporal punishment is usually avoided by the Kalinga since this may lead
to reprisals or demands for the payment of fines by angry relatives. If a Kalinga lays
a hand on a child, the parents, out of a sense of pride and the urge to preserve traditional customs, must revenge or demand the payment of indemnities. No action is
taken on a non-Kalinga who, in a recognized position of authority, employs corporal punishment. Indeed, parents might even express their gratitude to such a person
for giving their child "proper training."

The Kalinga have strong negative feelings about twins. In the past, one of
the pair, the one judged the most frail, was usually exposed to perish while the
stronger one was permitted to survive. Sometimes parents would "deceive" the spirits by pretending to abandon one of the twins but recovering it later, or by changing the name of one of them after a time. Another method was to give one of the
twins to a relative to raise. The reason for the taboo on twins is unknown, but it is
probably related to the difficulty of nursing two infants at once under the former
subsistence economy of swidden farming.

In Lubuagan, it was customary in the past for boys to be circumcised at
about the age of seven. A number of old men without any special position in the
society had the knowledge to perform the operation. Which one of these men was
selected to circumcise a particular boy was up to his parents. The "surgeon" received a small payment either in produce, materials, or money. The man who performed the operation abstained from eating taro until after the operation healed;
otherwise, there was no prescribed ritual associated with circumcision. The operation is rarely performed anymore in Lubuagan, although it has been reported that
circumcision was once characteristic of all the Kalinga south of the Pacil River. In-

formants all denied that circumcision was ever performed in the northern Kalinga areas, although informants from the north knew that Southern Kalinga boys underwent the operation.

From ages four through ten, boys and girls play a variety of games. Perhaps the most common is a simple hide-and-seek game played in the evening by both girls and boys, either of one sex alone or as a mixed group. For boys, spinning tops is perhaps most popular; boys aged seven to fifteen play the game. Top games are not played by girls. There are also many unorganized games. Every village has a stream and a pool nearby where women get water and where clothes are washed. Here, children from three to ten years old bathe, swim and play games while women relatives wash clothes, scour pots and pans, and perform other household tasks.

The Kalinga delight in performing tasks which bring attention upon themselves as individuals. We will discuss later the exhibitionist qualities of adults, but children learn early to strive for activities which will make themselves visible. Plays and skits are popular and parents plan recitations for children to perform at public gatherings. The themes of these performances often come from their own school experiences. A poem or a piece of prose learned by a parent when a child, perhaps under an American school teacher, is taught to a young son or daughter. The child recites the poem at a peacepact gathering or at a regional festive gathering with dramatic vocal emphases and exaggerated hand gestures. There is always considerable applause, which reinforces the strong drive for individual achievement and distinction.

Beginning about the age of six or seven, boys and girls tend to separate themselves. The relations between brothers and sisters become those of respect, almost of avoidance. While distantly related boys and girls may tease and throw stones at one another, a brother and sister will not align themselves on opposing sides in such groups. The respect patterns continue into adulthood.

In Lubuagan and in the southern Kalinga area generally, girls in their teens usually sleep together in the homes of widows while boys sleep in vacant houses. This is not an invarient pattern, however, since some girls and boys prefer to remain in their own homes at night. The predominant sleeping arrangements of Southern Kalinga teenagers is known among the Northern Kalinga, who strongly disapprove of such a custom. In the north, boys and girls remain in their own houses at night, unless they are visiting a distant hamlet and decide to remain the night.

Contract Marriages

Arranged marriages were reported to be more prevelant in the past, although free choice of marriage partners apparently always existed as an option. A genealogical survey of marriages and other data for the Poswoy region indicated about half of the marriages had been contracted; the marriage partners of another one-fourth of the marriages had been contracted to marry others but had broken the contracts for one reason or another; while another one-fourth had married through free choice. Although samples were not taken from other areas, both Northern and Southern Kalinga informants indicated that these ratios seemed reasonably representative for the two cultural areas of Kalinga.

It was also reported that formerly, individuals rarely broke marriage contracts, whereas at present, there is an increasing tendency to break them. This statement is undoubtedly true. American attitudes toward marriage have diffused widely throughout the Mountain Province. Missions, boarding schools, recent opportunities for wage work, and trade are all factors which have weakened the custom of arranged marriages.

Northern Kalinga parents of a girl try to comply with contractual arrangements once begun more than do those of Lubuagan. This is probably because the boy's parents in the north contribute more gifts—which actually amounts to a bride price—than in Lubuagan, where the gifts exchanged between the two families is about equal.

While Kalinga parents use force occasionally, they are not as severe in enforcing marriages as elsewhere in the Mountain Province. Among the Ibaloy of Benguet Province, for example, the go-between who makes the arrangements for marriage uses rather drastic measures to consummate a marriage where the girl opposed. He strips the clothes off the girl, then binds her in a room and sends in her betrothed to have sex relations with her. If both object to the marriage, they are stripped of their clothes, bound together in a carabao hide and placed together in a locked room (Leaño 1958 :79–80).

Once it is common knowledge among the Kalinga that a girl has gone through the *ingilin* stage where the contracted couple sleep together, the marriage contract is considered consummated, although the final distribution of gifts and the wedding feast will not take place for another five months. No man would court a girl who has passed through this stage of the marriage contract. This is because such a man would be required to pay back all of the gifts exchanged between the two families through the years and he would be fined for making overtures to a girl whose marriage was already considered consummated. Hence, men will have nothing to do with a girl who has gone through the *ingilin* stage of the marriage contract. It is important to emphasize that the avoidance of a girl who has passed through this stage of the marriage contract is not for moral reasons, but because of the practical and economic difficulties involved in the situation. If a man tried to marry such a girl, it would be tantamount to making advances to a married woman and he would be inciting the wrath of two extended families, the girl's and the contracted partner's. The ordinary Kalinga man, though he may be interested in a contracted girl, would have nothing to do with one who has gone through this crucial stage of the marriage contract.

The details of contract marriages vary considerably from region to region, but such marriages do have a similar overall pattern. The one described here is specifically that for the region of Poswoy. Children are engaged soon after they are born. Ideally, the boy should be a year or so older than the girl. Both the girl's and the boy's family make sure beforehand by various subtle overtures that the planned engagement meets the approval of both parties. The boy's parents make the initial overt advances in arranging the marriage contract. They select a man or two men related to both parties to act as go-betweens (*manggogod* or *mambaga*). The mediators observe all omens and proceed to the girl's house only if all signs are favorable. Once at the house, traditional omens are again observed and a pig is killed and its bile sac examined for the proper favorable sign. If everything goes well, the mediators present the parents of the girl with valuable beads, *masilap* and *abali*. A feast is celebrated in the presence of the girl's relatives and the mediators are treated as honored guests. Upon leaving, they are presented with gifts for themselves and the forefront of the pig as a present to the boy's parents.

The acceptance of the beads and the feast, called *banat,* is the first step in the contractual arrangement. After the *banat,* the parents of the boy and the girl are invited to all feasts given by either set of parents and are given meat shares.

When the boy is between twelve and fourteen, he is taken to the girl's house by his relatives, who again observe all the omens and taboos ordinarily prescribed for the beginning of a crucial journey. In the girl's home, the boy performs services such as hauling fuel, working in the fields, and such other duties as may be required of him. Occasionally he may go home, remain for a few days and then return to the house of his betrothed. This custom, a form of bride service, is called *magngotogaw.*

About the age of seventeen or eighteen, the boy is again formally escorted to the girl's house. This is the final journey to the girl's home and will culminate in marriage. The relatives who escort the boy may be aunts or first cousins, but never the parents of the boy. If parents accompany the boy, it is feared that the spirits will believe that the parents are tired of their own son and want to get rid of him and hence bring illness or misfortune to the members of the escorting party. This formal escort preceding the series of events that terminate in marriage is called *tolód.* All of the omens are carefully observed and if these are unfavorable, the journey may be postponed for a day or more until they are favorable. If the marriage is to be between partners from different regional units, a group of men playing the *pantángkog* (bamboo sticks struck against each other) precedes the escorting party. The *tolód* is also performed for marriages resulting from individual choice when the groom joins his bride immediately preceding marriage.

The arrival of the escorting party is an occasion for feasting. The boy's relatives are feted and return with gifts for themselves and the boy's parents. When they leave they carry back with them the forefront of the pig butchered for the occasion. Shares of meat from the pig will be distributed to all of the relatives of the boy. This occasion is called *kagítkit* in Poswoy.

About two weeks later, valuable gifts are given by the boy's family to the girl. These gifts usually consist of sixty precious Chinese beads and about twenty Chinese plates. After this gift-giving, the boy and girl may sleep together as husband and wife. This stage of the marriage ceremony is called *ingilin.*

The official fulfillment of the marriage contract occurs five months after the *ingilin.* This is the wedding feast celebrated in all regions of Kalinga, although the designation of the feast varies considerably. In Lubuagan it is called *togtogaw;* in

Salegseg, *among;* and in Poswoy, *pasingan.* At this time, relatives from both sides of the couple's families through third cousins are invited to the feast and receive meat shares of carabaos killed for the occasion. A basket of gifts called *gala* is given by the boy's relatives and another by the girl's relatives to the couple. The relatives are extremely competitive in this gift-giving, each set attempting to outdo the other by contributing the most precious and valuable gifts. At this time, too, the *banbansak* is decided. This represents the gifts given by the boy's relatives to the girl's relatives. The most valuable gifts, such as Chinese jars, carabaos and rice fields go to the eldest brother, parents and grandparents of the girl, while the girl's more distant relatives, such as first and second cousins, receive Chinese plates and money. The amounts given to the girl's relatives, of course, depend on the wealth of the boy's relatives. Wedding feasts are highly competitive affairs, each kinship group attempting to display its bountiful economic resources. Among the Northern Kalinga where the bulk of the gifts is contributed by the boy's relatives, the wedding feast highlights particularly the wealth and prestige of the boy's kindred.

At the time of the wedding feast, the parents of the couple also give their daughter or son a part of their share of the family inheritance. This consists of rice fields, carabaos, Chinese jars, plates, beads and the like with which the couple may set up their own household. The inherited property collectively is called *tawid.* Since the *ingilin,* the couple have been living with the girl's parents, but after the wedding feast a separate residence is constructed for them. Residence among the Northern Kalinga is statistically only slightly uxorilocal.

The wedding feast lasts for a day and night. Sugar cane wine is consumed in large quantities while two or more gong orchestras take turns in providing music for the dances. Prominent men boast of their war records or of their economic resourcefulness.

Variations in the pattern of the Kalinga contractual marriage custom as described for Poswoy are evident in the different regions. Crucial features which appear to be present in all areas, however, are the following: (1) selection of a go-between or go-betweens by the boy's parents; (2) formal visit of these mediators to the girl's parents, the presentation of a gift and their return with gifts for themselves and the boy's parents; (3) formal escort of the boy to the girl's home shortly before the marriage feast; and (4) a marriage feast with the exchange of gifts between the girl's and boy's relatives.

Uncontracted Marriages

While a considerable number of Kalinga marriages result from the betrothal of infants, individual choice of marriage partners also exists. As we have noted, in about one-fourth of Poswoy marriages there had been no betrothal of either partner and in about another one-fourth neither partner had been contracted; hence, about one-half of Poswoy marriages were contracted by individual choice. Since a definite courting pattern exists among the Kalinga, we may assume that the individual choice of marriage partners is also an old practice.

Arrangements for a boy and a girl to see one another is made by themselves; it is not customary to employ a go-between in arranging a meeting. If a boy is interested in a girl, he finds an opportunity to intercept the girl on her way to fetch water or to catch her attention at a public gathering. The initial contact is extremely subtle, for Kalinga etiquette forbids girls and boys to talk to one another in the open. A boy constantly seeks occasions on which he can catch the eye of the girl in whom he is interested. A vague sign unnoticed by others such as a subtle wink, a raised eyebrow, or the sudden lowering of the eyes with a faint smile might be indicative that the boy has found favor in the girl. Emboldened by such a sign of approval, the boy will present himself at the girl's home in the evening. The boy prepares special courting songs, *olalim* or *balagoyos,* and practices on the lip flute, *paldong,* and nose flute, *tongali,* and then serenades and woos his girl friend.

If the arrangement is satisfying to both the girl and the boy, the girl may arrange to see the boy under more private circumstances when her parents are away. Among the Southern Kalinga, where girls customarily sleep in the houses of widows, he may visit her there at night. In time, the couple decides to marry; their parents are informed and a date is set for the marriage feast. The girl's parents give the first feast and are hosts to the groom's parents and his kindred. This feast is later followed in some regions by a similar one given by the groom's parents, the latter acting as hosts. After this ceremony, the couple is considered married and takes up residence as described above for contract marriages.

Mistresses

Taking up with a mistress, *dagdagas,* is condoned, but permission of parents is usually necessary. A man gives beads or other objects of value to a woman who has consented to be his mistress. Children of mistresses are entitled to some of a man's inheritance, although they do not receive as much as a man's children from his legitimate wife. In the event that a man has no children from his legal wife, then his children from his mistress will inherit as if they were his own. A son may have a *dagdagas* when still a bachelor but the permission of his parents is essential in such a case. Under any circumstance, it is good to have the permission of parents for the eventual disposal of inheritance property may then be anticipated and taken into account by the latter in the event that there are children from such a union. It is important to emphasize that no child, whether of a legal union or of a mistress, is denied support or inheritance rights. The prominent leaders of a region, *pangats,* see to it that every child is properly cared and provided for. A wife does not object if her husband takes a mistress when she is old or if she is barren. Indeed, a barren woman might ask a man to take a mistess so that one or more of the children by her husband and his mistress may be raised as their own and hence inherit their property. Mistresses are often women of villages other than a man's own. Peace pact holders and traders often take mistresses in the villages of the regions with which they have pacts and conduct trade. Much more rarely, a prominent and wealthy man might take a mistress in his own town, a practice almost completely restricted to the more densely populated communities of the south. In the latter case, the relationship is apparently fully condoned by the wife as the mistress then becomes a kind of second wife under the domination of the legal wife. The mistress is housed nearby with her children (if any) and helps the wife with her household duties. Should the first wife die during the time the husband has this type of *dagdagas* relationship, then the mistress attains full and accepted status as a wife.

Prostitutes are said not to exist anywhere among the Kalinga. Detailed census data and occupational information on individuals obtained for the regions of Poswoy and Mabaca revealed no prostitutes. While comparable data was not compiled for any of the regions in southern Kalinga, Lubuagan informants were emphatic that there were no prostitutes in the southern Kalinga regions.

There is no clear distinction between adopted children and servants. Well-to-do families have one or more servants, although they are most common in the densely populated communities of the south. An adopted child is called *inanak* and a servant, *poyong,* but the treatment accorded to either seems not to differ markedly. Indeed, adopted children and servants become, in most respects, like other children of the household. They receive a portion of their foster parents' inheritance, although not as much as actual children. They are well treated and Kalinga custom law extends protective controls over them in the same manner as toward other individuals. Adopted children are usually orphaned relatives, while servants come from poorer families. If a servant comes from another region, the peace pact regulations of both regions protect the individual. The physical safety of the servant is thus even more secure than that of other individuals. Servants receive no compensation for their services, but are usually in better circumstances than they would be in their natal homes since only better-situated families can afford to keep them. An adopted child may be contracted in marriage like an actual child, but a *poyong* must seek a wife on his own initiative, or if a girl, become a wife by individual choice. A girl servant often becomes a mistress. As a mistress or a wife, she loses her special status as a servant and her husband or lover must provide for her or compensate her in the same manner as any other woman. Adopted children and servants, like other members of a region, have the right to appeal to regional *pangats* for inheritance of property and adjudication of wrongs suffered either from their masters or from others. All individuals, whatever their socioeconomic or personal status, appear to be treated fairly and equally among the Kalinga everywhere (Barton 1949:64–65).

Divorce

Divorces have a high correlation with childless marriages. If a couple does not have a child in a year or two, they almost certainly will separate. Some childless couples remain married by adopting a child, either a son or a daughter of a relative, or in more rare cases, a child born of the union of the husband and his mistress. The Northern Kalinga, who are perhaps more sensitive to the Roman Catholic priest's admonitions, rarely present themselves to be married by him until a wife is well along in pregnancy, or may even wait until after a child is born. This is because the Catholic priest emphasizes the permanence of marriages which he performs and the Kalinga realize that only when a child has arrived, or is safely on the way, can a marriage be considered a permanent venture. A child is essential for the stability of every marriage, and the *banbansak* (Northern Kalinga) or *atod* (Southern Kalinga), which designates the custom of gift-giving by the groom's to the bride's relatives, does not take place until the couple have lived as husband and wife for about five months and the wife is pregnant.

In Poswoy, the majority of those individuals who had been divorced one or more times (approximately 50 percent of the population), had divorced because they had had no children in their previous unions. Divorces for reasons other than lack of children is rare; it was reported, however, that a man might divorce a wife if she were not pleasant and hospitable to his guests. Kalinga culture places high value on hospitality, and girls are taught from early childhood to be gracious hosts to visitors. There are few wives, therefore, who are not mindful of this highly valued precept. A wife who is sullen and unpleasant to her husband's guests, whether relatives or friends, suffers censure not only from her husband but from the whole society. Industry and hard work are other traits that are given high value in Kalinga culture, and the rare wife who is lacking these qualities is unlikely to remain married for long. Other factors such as adultery or the *dagdagas* system appear to be negligible in divorces. Perhaps because of the custom of infant betrothal, early marriage, and the mistress system, promiscuity in women or the incidence of adultery by either men or women is not a serious problem. The rather severe penalties imposed by custom law on those who transgress the accepted sexual privileges provided by marriage and the *dagdagas* relationship may also be a deterrent to adulterous and promiscuous behavior. A man has the right to punish his wife severely and even to kill her should she be caught in the act of adultery. The case of a man who commits adultery or seduces an unmarried girl is taken before the regional leaders who impose heavy fines, and if a child is born of the relationship, the man is required to support the child and set aside a portion of his inheritance property for the child.

Adult Life and Occupational Activities

After marriage, men and women enter actively into adult life. The normal and continuous work of men involves the clearing of swiddens and the plowing of rice fields. Although men work hard at these tasks, their work is ordinarily confined to daylight hours. This is in striking contrast to the duties of women, whose work begins in the dark of early morning and continues far into the night. In the village, unless a house is under construction, men loll around or are assembled together in loud and boisterous conversation. During the dry season, after the rice harvest in January and before the clearing of swiddens in March, men travel about extensively. This is the time of peace pact celebrations when men have the opportunity to trade and buy, and if skillful, to advance the economic well-being of their households and thus bring prestige to their kinship groups.

There is little change at present in the pattern of activities for a man from a young married adult to old age. Prestige and status is advanced primarily by increasing land holdings, the acquisition of pigs and carabaos and the accumulation of heirlooms in the form of Chinese plates, jars and gongs. To this must be added large lowland-type houses with galvanized roofs. Those who acquire these possessions are men of the *baknang* class to which every married man aspires.

Pangats (*lakays, capitánes*) are usually men of the *baknang* class, but a man of means does not automatically become a member of this distinguished group. An informal, tacit acceptance of the individual by the regional population is the only road to "pangathood." This is a long process. There is no formal vote taken; people "just know" who have arrived at that point where they may be considered influential regional leaders. A man of wealth who wants to enter this privileged class must speak up in regional festivals; he must argue wisely, eloquently and at length the cases of his home region at peace pact meetings. No man is barred from speaking at Kalinga gatherings, but public reaction to any comment or speech, whether favorable or unfavorable, is unmistakable to a Kalinga spectator. A man who speaks often and who receives the respectful attention of an audience may be said to be along the road to becoming a *pangat*. If, in addition, such an individual begins to be sought for his advice in time of trouble and the news gets around that he gives wise counsel, another step in the right direction may be said to have been taken. As a man of means matures, continues to speak eloquently and wisely at gatherings, counsels often and in keeping with the fundamentals of custom law, sooner or later people will begin to address him as *pangat, lakay,* or *capitán*. When this happens, he has arrived at that point where he is a member of this informal but influential fraternity.

The *pangats* do not meet as a formal body and certainly they cannot be considered in any sense a council. They do often discuss regional problems but these occur informally at regional festivals where the men of influence lounge around together. On such occasions, while squatting and chewing betel nut and discoloring the ground with their spittle, they talk for long hours. They discuss regional troubles and cases which have been brought before them. Each leader presents his views on the subject, usually by citing precedents from similar cases previously settled, but always injecting his own personal opinions on the matter. It is in such situations that the regional leaders sample public opinion, which will be considered carefully by each one when called upon by relatives in trouble.

In settling actual cases, the regional leader or leaders operate more as arbiters than as formal judges. Any trouble, such as theft, a physical injury, or a case of adultery, is taken immediately by the injured party to a *pangat* who is related to his kinship group. In the meantime, the offender has done likewise, consulting a man of influence who is related to his kinship group. The immediate reaction of the regional leaders is to advise moderation and caution against hasty, unreasonable action. Each leader will look into the case at once, calling upon the older and most respected members of each kinship group. Eventually the two *pangats* involved

The small hamlet of Pepe in the Salegseg region (northern Kalinga). The tin-roofed structure is the home of a regional leader (lakay).

in the case will meet. In such a meeting the highest qualities of diplomacy are exercised. Each regional leader is careful not to offend or arouse the ire of the other and the use of personal compliments is profuse. The preliminaries may take several days before a decision is reached. In the meantime, some regional festival will have taken place—a wedding, a sickness rite, or a funeral. Here each of the leaders involved will have an opportunity to discuss the case, listening attentively to the opinion of other leaders. On the basis of these discussions and on the precedent set by other similar cases in the past, an "amicable settlement" will be decided.

While a man becomes a member of this privileged class by leadership and business acumen, some have entered the class by accidental circumstances. A number of Kalinga men were fortunate to be recognized as aiding the war effort by participating as guerrilla fighters during the Japanese occupation. These individuals receive United States government checks and are also entitled to buy American goods in the U.S. government commissary at Camp John Hay in Baguio. The goods they buy are promptly sold at increased prices in black market establishments in Baguio. While the amounts such individuals realize from government checks and commissary products they sell are minimal in terms of United States economy, they represent small fortunes among the Kalinga.

Modern conditions have brought about important changes in positions that determine status and distinction among men. It is no longer possible at present to become renowned as a courageous warrior, *mangol*. Education is now considered to be an essential step to most positions for which one would strive. While a few illiterate old men still retain important status positions as regional leaders, young *pangats* or *lakays* are those who can read, write, and speak English. Schooling in other positions is even more important. In Balbalan district, which embraces most of northern Kalinga, individuals who hold positions from barrio lieutenants to the municipal mayor may be literate in English. To be a schoolteacher, an occupation which appeals to the young Kalinga, a teacher's certificate is required which cannot be attained in less than two or three years of schooling beyond high school.

Beginning in the mid-eighteenth century, some men became part-time traders, although no one became exclusively a trader. Other occupational tasks performed by men, such as blacksmithing and basket-weaving, were also part time. The weaving of cotton cloth and the making of pottery were women's occupations, also on a part-time basis. Thus, there were no full-time specialists among either men or women.

The Kalinga in the past was mainly a subsistence farmer, in early times growing rice in swiddens and in more recent years shifting to irrigated rice. At present, an increasing number of individuals are becoming wage workers, either as municipal employees or as laborers, in Baguio and other cities of Luzon. The bulk of the Kalinga populations, however, continues as subsistence farmers.

Women not only assist their men with farm work, but do all of the work around the house: nursing and caring for children, pounding and winnowing rice, preparing meals, scouring floor mats, and carrying water. During feasts and the visits of friends and relatives, they accelerate the normal activities of housework and must, in addition, appear as smiling and gracious hostesses. The lot of a wife of a prominent man is considerably harder, although such women do occasionally have extra help. In the homes of the *baknang,* there is almost a continuous series of visitors who must be fed and entertained. These occasions, called *palános,* help to promote and maintain the position of influential leaders and to elevate the status of their kinship groups. While the men of the extended household circulate among the guests, women are cooking and serving food and *basi* (sugarcane wine). After the *palános,* men of the kindred segment in the village may lounge around outside, receiving the congratulations of neighbors for having given an elaborate feast and providing gracious hospitality to the visitors. But the work of women goes on; they wash and scour to prepare the house again to receive guests, always ready to serve and provide generous welcome to the friends of their menfolk.

The only semiprofessional positions for women among the Kalinga are as curers or mediums. Mediums come nearer to being full-time specialists. A woman becomes a medium not by individual choice or inclination but by being psychologically disposed to it. The Kalinga believe that mediums are selected by the spirits. A woman thus "called" exhibits peculiar food and behavior habits recognized by the Kalinga as summons to assume the role of a medium (see Chapter 3). In the regions visited, mediums are all women past the age of thirty. In Poswoy, a region of approximately 500 inhabitants, informants reported that there were about a dozen mediums.

In addition to mediums, a few women (three were reported in Poswoy) become specialists in the treatment of women who have trouble bearing children or wish to abort after conception. These women are not midwives; the Kalinga apparently do not have midwives. Women of an extended household, usually the mother, assist at childbirth. Should there be difficulty at birth, one of these childbirth specialists is called. The primary function of the curer is, then, to help a barren woman conceive, to assist in difficult births, and to perform abortions. Such work is always conducted on a part-time basis; most of the time these women carry on their normal duties as housewives.

In recent years, women have been able to get into other nontraditional positions. These women work as schoolteachers and municipal clerks, jobs for which schooling beyond the high school is required. Schooling receives high value in Kalinga culture, and the desire to achieve an education will undoubtedly lead more and more men and women into professions new to traditional Kalinga society and culture. But for a society still engaged predominantly in subsistence farming and which stresses periodic prestige feasts and generous hospitality to frequent visitors, the lot of most women will continue to be characterized by hard work both in the fields and at home.

Men and women during the course of their lives will very likely become involved at least once in some kind of litigation proceedings within their own region. Kalinga custom law consists of a remarkably large body of jural procedures known to most adults but about which the *pangats* or regional arbiters are especially knowledgeable. Since there are so many infractions which require litigation, it is virtually impossible for a Kalinga, or some member of his kinship group, to escape involvement in the Kalinga jural system.

In settling disputes and assessing fines and indemnities, the arbiters make pronouncements which are usually accepted as the proper interpretation of custom law. Such interpretations, however, are always made by regional leaders only after a careful survey of public opinion on the matter, and thus their judgments are rarely in conflict with group feeling.

Illness

Every individual will likely become ill or suffer an injury at some time during the course of his life. On such occasions the services of the medium and curer are engaged, and animals are sacrificed to appease ancestral and malevolent spirits. The number of animals sacrificed varies with the age and importance of the patient. Sickness rites for prominent individuals in the grandparent generation are most elaborate. When a grandparent of the wealthy class is seriously ill, the rites reach the proportions of a celebration. Relatives of the patient through the third cousins attend and receive shares of meat distributed by a *pangat*.

If all the efforts of the medium and curer fail and the patient dies, a relative goes outside and shouts the news. The information is relayed quickly throughout the region to members of the victim's kinship circle.

Funeral Rites

Funerals are more elaborate in the Lubuagan region and more subdued in the north, but even in the latter regions, they are festive occasions rather than somber and sad affairs. Among all Kalinga a wake is conducted and the sacrifices are offered in order to honor the spirit of the deceased and to ask him to accept the sacrifices and not bring misfortune and illness to the living.

Children are buried near the house or under granaries. Formerly, in the northern Kalinga areas, there was secondary burial of the bones of adults in jars. Adults are most commonly buried in graves about 6 feet deep and 3 feet wide, lined in the bottom and sides with small rocks and smoothed over with lime plaster. Large slabs of flat rock are placed on top of the corpse and the rest of the pit filled with dirt. A thatch-roofed arbor supported by four bamboo poles is then erected over the grave. At present, some Kalinga bury their dead in concrete tombs; this is especially characteristic of the well-to-do in the Lubuagan region. Such tombs contain the remains of several individuals; they are rather large and are properly family tombs.

In Poswoy, *gongwoy* (betel-nut preparation), charcoal, and lemon leaves are placed on top of the grave or tomb. Giant ghouls, *alan* or *kotmó,* who seek to feed on corpses are believed to be repelled by these objects. A food offering in the form of rice bread is also hung from the thatch-roofed ceiling above the grave or tomb in Poswoy. Also in Poswoy, nine days after burial, all the personal belongings of the deceased such as a spear, headaxe, raincoat, digging stick, or bolo, are placed on the grave. A man's belongings are put in a carrying pack, those of a woman in a basket.

Mourning and food taboos are strictly observed, in all areas of Kalinga, by the closely related kin of the deceased. For about a month in Poswoy, a surviving spouse (*pangis,* man; *bilog,* woman) cannot eat meat, fresh-water fish, or root foods; his or her diet must be restricted to fruits and vegetable greens. During this time, they are also forbidden to pick fruit and to cook their own food. The sacrifice of a chicken about a month after the death of one's spouse removes the food taboos and the restriction on cooking and picking fruit, by mourning continues for another year. A spouse cannot marry for a year, and together with other members of the household, he or she is required to observe the following restrictions: dancing and singing is prohibited; a strip of black or brown cloth must be wrapped around the forehead, arm, or chest; both sexes must let their hair grow freely and not oil it.

Approximately a year after the death of a parent or grandparent, a ceremony or celebration called *koliás* is given which ends the mourning period and removes all the restrictions from the household members. *Koliás* is a big feast where one or more large animals are butchered and served to relatives, neighbors and friends. The number of animals butchered and the size of the feast prepared depends on the wealth of the household and closely related kin—the wealthier, the more elaborate will be the *koliás*. There is dancing, and songs are sung. The first to dance is the father of the deceased, followed by the widow or widower, and then the other members of the household. There is also the recital of war exploits by those who have killed, and the recounting of outstanding achievements and accomplishments by wealthy and prominent individuals. The *koliás* is approximately a twenty-four hour affair, beginning in the morning of one day and ending in the morning of the second day.

In all Kalinga areas the mourning period for a child under the age of one is only about a month. Mourning is further extended for older children, and for adults it is ordinarily no less than a year. For all deaths, there is a feast to remove behavioral and food restrictions, although the age and importance of the individual will determine when the mourning will be terminated. The older the deceased was at his death and the greater his prominence, the longer will be the mourning period and the more elaborate will be the *koliás*.

Formerly, a man whose son or parent died went to another region to hunt for a head. It was the belief of the Kalinga that one life atones for another, and that taking the life of an enemy pleased the spirits and would keep the spirits from sending misfortune to the living. If a man brought back a head, he was welcomed with an elaborate celebration in which he danced. A successful headhunting expedition was believed to remove all sorrow over his loss and ended mourning.

The *koliás* ends the mourning period and is also believed to remove the sorrow of losing a near and beloved one. Crying and continuing despondency over one's loss after the *koliás* is considered very bad and likely to produce another death. A man or woman who cannot be consoled in his sorrow is asked to exhume the bones of the deceased and wash and rebury them, or else to take a journey on which a large river is crossed. Such acts are believed to be effective in restoring a sorrowing and despondent individual to normal life.

The above discussion of the life cycle highlights the importance of birth, marriage, sickness, and death as especially important occasions in the life of an individual. In the past, headhunting activities were also emphasized, especially for young adults, but ritual headhunting is now a thing of the past. In part, peace pact celebrations have substituted for the activities previously associated with headhunting, but the peace pact meetings also serve other functions. They are now occasions for social interaction with people formerly considered the enemy.

Kalinga celebrations, whether associated with the life cycle or with peace pacts, are primarily social and prestige feasts. The religious significance of the animals butchered and the food served in these feasts as sacrificial offerings to the spirits, which may have formerly received greater emphasis, appears at present to be of secondary importance. Even the sickness and death rites are social events essentially reflecting prestige.

3

Religion—Ritual and Beliefs

RITUALISTIC PERFORMANCES show extreme variations in all the Kalinga areas and from one region to another. Indeed, even within the region there is variation in religious practices. The variation is due primarily to the isolation of regional populations, which has retarded diffusion, but the desire of the religious practitioners, or mediums themselves, constantly to introduce innovations has also contributed to ritualistic differences. The Kalinga medium has her own spirit helpers and she endeavors to bring novel techniques into her performance of the rituals in order to set herself apart from other mediums.

Despite variations, there are common patterns both in religious concepts and practices, not only among the Kalinga but among the pagan peoples of northern Luzon generally. As among nonliterate peoples everywhere, religious beliefs and practices have a close relationship with the form of subsistence, social organization, and values. Which is cause and which is effect is perhaps impossible to determine, but the correspondence of religious beliefs and practices with subsistence and other social and cultural features is an interesting phenomenon.

Religious Concepts

Disease, crop failure, death, and all misfortunes are attributed primarily to the machinations of spirits. Other causative agents, such as sorcery and the violation of taboos, are also offered to explain a particular illness or death, but generally any misfortune is thought to be brought about by spirits. These spirits may be those of deceased individuals, particularly those of close relatives, or they may be any of a host of malevolent spirits. Spirits are known as *anitos,* a designation used by virtually all mountain peoples and many Filipino lowland peoples as well.

When an individual dies, his soul or spirit must be properly dispatched to the afterworld and the rituals prescribed for the funeral carefully observed. The place of the afterworld is not too clearly conceived; some believe that the spirits of the dead simply hover about the neighborhood; others believe that there is a separate abode for them somewhere in the sky. Life on earth does not appear to affect existence in the hereafter except for suicides and those who have died in accidents or who have been killed in warfare. The spirits of such individuals are vengeful and might cause illness and death unless properly propitiated. But there are no rewards or punishments in the hereafter for the kind of life people have led on earth. Everywhere among the mountain people there is a belief that the spirit of the dead remains near the corpse until after the funeral and watches carefully to see that all the ritualistic observances are made. Should anything be neglected, the spirit will take vengeance on his own relatives by sending illness or death. While the deceased's spirit is most potent during the period immediately following death, it is still likely to inflict illness or death at a later period if demands are neglected. Requests for things that an ancestral spirit needs come in the form of dreams, but sickness in the family may also be a sign that the spirit of a dead ancestor wants something. In the latter case, the medium interprets the message and indicates the object or objects desired by the spirits. Requests are usually for the sacrifice of animals, but sometimes for specific items like a blanket, tobacco, and other utilitarian things which are then placed on the deceased's grave.

The nonhuman spirits who bring illness, death, or misfortune are variously designated and not too clearly conceptualized. Some of them are good spirits, although perhaps the majority are malevolent. Various precautions are taken to avoid the machinations of these spirits and the main task of religious practitioners is to placate and propitiate them by prayers and the sacrifice of chickens and pigs. Some of these nonhuman spirits are more powerful than others and are more active in their efforts to inflict harm on the living. For the weaker spirits or the good ones, the mountain peoples have little concern; their preoccupation is with those which are powerful and hence a source of evil. These malicious spirits must be constantly placated by elaborate and costly sacrifices.

The machinations of ancestral spirits appear to be emphasized in the south, particularly among the Ibaloy (Barton 1946:9–10; Leaño 1958:266) and Sagada (Eggan 1959). Among the Northern Kalinga and the Tinguian (Cole 1922:295–314) nonhuman malevolent spirits appear to be most important as causative agents of illness, death, and misfortune. The Southern Kalinga of the Lubuagan region appear to stand about midway in this respect. While the religion of the Ibaloy, the Kankanay of Sagada, and the Southern Kalinga might be considered a form of ancestor worship, at least in part, such a characterization would not be appropriate for the Northern Kalinga. The main preoccupation of the Northern Kalinga mediums is with malevolent spirits and the anxieties of the living, and with the machinations of the spirits which are evilly disposed. Except for funeral ceremonies and the observation of taboos during the mourning period, offerings are not made for the dead among the Northern Kalinga. It is possible that the importance of specific family lines among the suthern groups might be correlated with this difference in religious emphases. In Chapter 1, we have noted that bilateral descent groups are present in the south, but not among the Northern Kalinga. Given a belief in the power of ancestral spirits, it seems reasonable to expect that such spirits would be accorded greater attention where specific family lines are singled out. Just as adult members of important families exerted control over their relatives, so also they would be inclined to do so after death unless they were constantly appeased. The correlation here suggested is, of course, a conjectural one, but the crucial contrast between the two areas is the presence of bilateral descent groups and the emphases placed on ancestral spirits in one but not in the other.

In the central and southern portions of the Mountain Province, sorcery is frequently reported as a cause of illness and death (Leaño 1958; Barton 1919), but the Kalinga are skeptical about it and have little or no anxiety over witchcraft. Poisoning is, however, greatly feared and Kalinga attitudes toward poisoning often taken on a magical significance that is closely related to the concept of witchcraft. Thus, it is believed, for example, that injury, illness, or death can be brought to an individual by "poisoning" his clothing or other items which are constantly in contact with him. The most frequent method of poisoning is by introducing a poisonous preparation made from putrefied roots into drink or food. While this would be considered an act of true poisoning, the precautions to ward it off are magical. Throughout the Kalinga country individuals carry various kinds of amulets and preparations which are supposed to detect the poisoning of food or drink. A common preparation is the mixture of coconut oil and a certain type of root. The preparation is called *somang* or *soblay* in the Northern Kalinga dialects. *Soblay* is carried in a small bottle and when food or drink about to be eaten has been poisoned, oil oozes out of the bottle, thus alerting the carrier. Some informants report that the possession of preparations like *soblay* magically breaks the container of food or drink that has been poisoned. Old childless women are especially feared by the Kalinga as potential poisoners. Such women are said to be seeking revenge for their condition and would entice a traveler into their homes to poison him with food or drink.

The violation of taboo is believed to be a cause of illness, death, or misfortune, and may be associated with ancestral or malevolent spirits. The omission of necessary details in the performance of ceremonies, or the disregard of prohibitive regulations during birth and early childhood ceremonies, or at times of planting, harvesting, and other important occasions, may result in evil consequences. The spirits who reside in the *podayan*, a small shelter at the entrance of a village, are easily offended if villagers do not pay proper respect to the guardian stones called *bayog* contained therein. *Sangásang*, considered to be the powerful guardian spirit of the village and formerly associated with warfare, lives in the *podayan*. If this shrine is violated, the guardian spirit of the village will take vengeance by sending some kind of calamity; hence proper respect must be displayed at the shrine. A small glass of wine or an egg in a bowl should be offered periodically to the village guardian spirit.

Almost all the mountain peoples venerate a creator-deity or culture hero or both. Virtually everywhere among the Kalinga there is simply one such creator god called *kabónyan* or *kaboníyan*. This deity is directly appealed to only in rare cases such as when a man has lost a loved one through death or accident, or when a man has suffered a sudden calamity such as the destruction of his rice fields by a storm.

On such an occasion a man might exclaim: "*Kaboníyan,* look thou upon me and have pity for see what has been taken from me!" *Kaboníyan* is not invoked by the mediums, however. Each medium has her own spirit helpers to whom she appeals when performing a ceremony. The Kalinga and other Mountain Province peoples appear to propitiate only those spirits which can harm; since *kaboníyan* does not inflict injury, bring sickness or misfortune, there is no need to placate or appease him. In their attitude toward spirits and deities the practical, self-interested characteristics of the mountain peoples are highlighted: "Why exert time, energy, and use up one's economic resources in sacrificial feasts for benevolent spirits and a good deity? Those ancestral and malevolent spirits who bring about illness, death, and misfortune are the ones who need to be compromised."

Categories of Ritualistic Activity

The areas of human activity emphasized by ritualistic activity are much the same among all of the Mountain Province peoples. They center about the life cycle, agriculture, and headhunting. Headhunting ritual is still vividly remembered by the Kalinga, but the energy formerly devoted to headhunting activities and the celebration that marked the return of a headhunting expedition has been rechanneled into the popular peace pact celebrations.

Ritual associated with the life cycle and agriculture still goes on, but such rites have diminished in intensity and frequency as the result of nontraditional governmental and missionary influences. Mountain Province peoples highlight those stages in the life cycle of the individual which are potentially dangerous. Among the Kalinga, special rites, the *kontad* series, bridge the child over the period when it is most vulnerable to the machinations of the spirits. The child is unable to protect himself at this time, so parents and close relatives must observe the taboos which, if transgressed, would harm the child. They bribe and buy off by sacrificial offerings the malevolent and ancestral spirits which may take advantage of the child's vulnerability. While *kontad* rites are specifically of the Kalinga, they are much the same in all groups. Marriage ceremonies emphasize prestige and status drives practically everywhere, but there is recognition, too, of the entrance of the individual into a new life and a new set of relationships. Finally, the ritualistic activities associated with death stem out of kinship ties between the living and the deceased, but the relatives who conduct the ceremonies also have practical and mundane interests in performing these rites. The bontiful and lavish offerings express not only an affectionate attachment of living relatives for the deceased but there is also the desire to impress others by the very elaborateness of the ceremony. In this final aspect, the Kalinga are perhaps most obviously worldly and exhibitionistic, emphasizing more than the other groups the prestige features of all of these ritualistic events.

The ceremonial activities that are observed in connection with agriculture vary to the extent that basic subsistence patterns differ. These activities also reflect historical circumstances, that is, the persistence of certain practices fitted to earlier forms of subsistence and agricultural techniques. Thus, the ritualistic attention given to the planting of taro among the Kankanay at Sagada and Bontoc (Eggan 1959; Jenks 1905) appears to indicate a shift from the primary cultivation of wet taro (now insignificant in the diet of these people) to irrigated rice. Among the Kalinga the cultivation of dry rice receives emphasis although wet rice is now of equal or even of major importance.

The concepts associated with headhunting, despite obvious differences in ritualistic practices, again appear to be much the same everywhere among the Kalinga. Headhunting apparently satisfied primarily prestige and status needs of the mountain peoples. The conversion of the rituals formerly associated with headhunting into community welfare interests indicates that a secondary function of headhunting rituals was an attempt to fortify magically the village or region against enemy attacks. Community solidarity was, of course, reinforced by headhunting activities,. and it is natural that with the cessation of these activities, the rituals were reorganized to emphasize community well-being. A further function of head hunting activities, especially for swidden farmers, was undoubtedly the maintenance of territorial space (Vayda 1961). Such a function is now obviated since Philippine governmental regulations of land tenure now determine limits of territorial expansion. Less clear as a possible alternative or subsidiary function of headhunting was its relevance to fertility. Early writers (Worcester 1912:833–930; Folkmar 1906; Barton 1949) were convinced that "bringing home a head brings general welfare, increases the fertility of fields, domestic animals, and women, and brings abundance of life generally" (Barton 1949:236). Informants, however, emphasize the prestige element for headhunting activities, although there is a commonly held belief that spilling human blood is a cure for childlessness. Another motive for headhunting is revenge or "evening the score." Thus, it was incumbent upon a young man to secure an enemy head when a near relative died, whatever the cause of death may have been. This act evened the score: "We lost one and the enemy lost one."

The Medium and the Placation of Spirits

The only professional position among the mountain peoples is that of the medium, *mangalisig* (Lubuagan Kalinga), *mandadawak, manganito* (Northern Kalinga). This position is nowhere a full-time occupation nor are there organizations of mediums with graded or specialized functions except incipiently among the Ifugao. Each medium, when she has learned the myths and the chants, embarks on her profession on a par with the others and retains her independent status. Mediums are most numerous among the central groups of the Mountain Province, particularly the Bontoc and the Ifugao. These groups have a long history of wet-rice cultivation and the activity of the mediums reflect this basic economy. The ceremonies of the Tinguian also involve the activities of mediums, but here the ceremonies and the mediums are concerned primarily with health and well-being. Among the Kalinga and the Isneg there are fewer mediums, ceremonies are less elaborate, and the mediums emphasize curing and headhunting rituals. Mediums are men among the Bontoc and Ifugao, whereas among the Tinguian, Isnegs, and among most of the Kalinga, they are women. Ifugao rituals appear to be an outlet for masculine exhibitionism; to a lesser extent, this is true of the Bontoc, but among Tinguian, Kalinga, and Apayao, men achieve distinction not as religious practitioners but in warfare or as mediators of troubles that arise from the infractions of custom law. Thus, if the Ifugao emphasize ritual activity over which priests preside, then the Kalinga and their neighbors excel as political manipulators. The profession of a medium is not closed to men among the northern groups, but these peoples feel that such positions are properly for women. Among the Kalinga, mediums are perhaps accorded the least distinction anywhere in the Mountain Province. Men frequently refer to them deprecatingly as "quack doctors," and informants are inclined to mask their importance, yet they will seek their services in time of illness or death.

Individuals cannot become mediums by choice; they must be "called." The Kalinga have a variety of symptoms which they interpret as summons to join the profession. Among the most important are disturbing dreams, trembling fits, and illness or nausea following the eating of certain kinds of foods, such as eel and dog. A Kalinga woman may resist the "summons" initially, but if the symptoms persist, she will seek out a medium and become her assistant, serving as a kind of apprentice. Over a period of several months, even over several years, she will learn the myths, the chants, and the names of a variety of deities and spirits. Much of this information she will have already acquired from being present at ceremonies where mediums officiate; hence, a medium's ritualistic performance would not be completely new to the novice. Under the instructions of an experienced medium, the novice will herself begin to summon spirits into herself. Sooner or later, if she is qualified and destined to become a medium, she will experience possession and out of a maze of spirits and deities who pass before her subconscious, some will appear more frequently and occupy her thoughts more persistently. Out of these she will eventually concentrate on three or four who will become her spirit helpers.

A Kalinga medium wears a turban, *bayobong,* made out of bark cloth and during the performance of a ceremony carries a Chinese plate which she rings with a bamboo stick as she chants. Other common materials used by the medium are the following: headaxe, coconut shells, tools like a grub hoe, and various types of ferns and hibiscus flowers. These items form a characteristic part of her ritual paraphernalia. At the end of her ritualistic performances, all these articles will be carefully collected and placed in a basket. While not all the items that make up the medium's ritual collections are the same, some, like the bark-cloth turban, the Chinese plate with bamboo stick, and the basket which contains these items, are all standard. A medium sacrifices a chicken in most rites, and for the major ones, for example those involving serious illnesses and funeral rites, the sacrificial victim is a pig or pigs. Ritualistic activities are conducted inside a dwelling. The medium's paraphernalia is deposited on a runo mat which serves as a kind of altar before which the medium sacrifices chickens or pigs and chants her prayers. Occasionally she may move about the room with the items on the mat but they are always returned to the mat. Kalinga ritual paraphernalia do not include wooden idols or sorcery boxes as among the Ifugao. Compared to the southern and central groups and the Tinguian, the ritual paraphernalia and the activities of the Kalinga medium are enormously simple, although they bear an obvious affinity to the Tinguian.

The Kalinga medium has no set fee for her services. As payment, she may receive the choicest part of the meat of the sacrificial victims, beads, money, clothes, or tools such as a headaxe, knife, or grub hoe. Such payment is never high and personal profit appears to have no part in the Kalinga medium's dedicated service. She is obligated to answer a request for her services regardless of when or by whom she is asked. A medium sincerely believes that she has been selected by certain spirits or deities to perform the ceremonies, and failure to carry out these responsibilities will have serious personal consequences. It is obvious, of course, that mediums derive considerable personal satisfaction from being the central focus of attention in ceremonies, but the profession is a demanding one. Kalinga mediums not only perform their share of women's work around the house and in the fields, but they also devote long and sleepless hours in ceremonies.

The activities of Kalinga mediums are similar to classic shamanistic performances the world over (compare Lowie 1954:161–164; Nadel 1946:25–37). Illness is believed to be the result of a temporary loss of the soul; restoration brings about a cure. Souls are "stolen" by the spirits of dead ancestors of the patient, although malevolent spirits may also steal a soul. If a soul is kept permanently, the victim dies. It is the task of the medium to bring the soul back and, hence, cure the patient. When called upon to treat a patient, the medium first determines whether the illness is caused by the spirit of an ancestor or ancestress or by other kinds of spirits. The medium sacrifices a chicken or pig, examines the liver of the animal and determines whether it is an auspicious time to enter the spirit world. If the sign is favorable, the liver is not spotted or marked; she then chants her prayers and summons her spirit helpers. As she chants, she appears to become sleepy and on the verge of falling asleep, yawning periodically. During one of these yawns (*manowob*), the name of the relative whose soul is causing the illness is emitted from her mouth. Upon regaining full consciousness, the medium will instruct the relatives how to placate the deceased relative and hence bring about recovery.

While there is considerable variation among the prayers sung by Kalinga mediums, and each medium has different spirit helpers, such prayers and the activities of the mediums in a ceremony do adhere to a similar pattern. Thus, ritualistic performances all have the following salient features:

(1) The medium begins her chanted prayer by invoking the deities or spirits collectively as *Apo!* (sir, master or lord).

(2) The medium lists her qualifications as the performer of the ceremony.

(3) She names her spirit helpers, usually three or more. Reports that the sacrificial victims are being offered for their needs.

(4) The medium is possessed by her spirit helpers. She is in a dazed, partly unconscious state. Other mediums may explain her chants if they are unintelligible.

(5) The medium goes into the spirit world to retrieve the spirit of the person (in a curing rite) or to communicate with the spirit world and try to answer the demands and questions of those who have come to attend the ceremony.

(6) The medium describes her experiences in the spirit world. She recovers

the spirit of the patient (in curing rites) and begins her journey back to the land of the living.

(7) The spirit or soul is returned to the patient and the medium regains consciousness.

(8) The medium and her medium helpers entertain the spectators by various skits.

(9) The medium gathers all of the things used in the ceremony, puts them in a basket and leaves the house without looking back.

The above outline has some of the same features covered by Ifugao rituals as listed by Barton (1946:4–6). Kalinga ritualistic performances also have many of the characteristics possessed by the Tinguian rituals. The name *dawak* is shared by the Northern Kalinga and Tinguian for the designation of the portion of a ceremony where the medium's spirit helpers are named, invoked, and possession takes place (Cole 1922:315). *Dawak* is a general term among the Northern Kalinga for the curing rite and mediums are designated as *mandadawak,* or the performers of *dawak.* The Tinguian have considerably more ceremonies than the Kalinga, but both groups emphasize sickness rites. The chants of the Tinguian mediums called *diams* (Cole 1915:5–6,26) are similar to those of the Northern Kalinga. The *diams,* which Cole designates as "stories dealing with the relations between certain persons and the natural spirits or those of the dead," are especially like the Northern Kalinga ritual chants (compare Cole 1915:27,183–189). Tinguian mediums and their activities also correspond. Practices differ considerably from the Ifugao, Sagada, and Bontoc. The religious practitioners of these groups are perhaps more properly priests, and several of them are involved in a ceremony. Kalinga ceremonies are performed by only one woman medium, occasionally by two or three, but never with as many as fifteen priests as among the Ifugao (Barton 1956:5).

The chanted or sung myths employed in rituals comprise a most important and widely distributed literary form among the mountain peoples. Among the Tinguian, Cole (1915:5) called them "explanatory myths." Cole so designated them because they are used to support or rationalize a ceremony (Barton 1956:3 for Ifugao). They are usually chanted only by mediums and generally occur in rituals, although there are some exceptions. Among the Northern Kalinga, some women, not mediums, chant special mythical folktales at harvest time or at night for diversion. These mythical folksongs are called *gosombi,* and they are sung as solos only by certain women.

The Nature of Kalinga Religion

Kalinga religion is based on a view of the supernatural world as antagonistic to the world of the living; the two worlds are opposed to each other. Supernaturals, whether the souls of spirits of the dead or spirits of beings who were never mortal, are malevolent and punitive. *Kaboniyan,* the culture hero, is an exception— a good god who never punishes. Yet the propitiatory activities of the Kalinga ignore *Kaboníyan* and consider him inconsequential or at least ineffective. A few isolated cases suggest that he is on rare occasions petitioned for help (compare Barton 1949:20), but the prayers, sacrifices and anxieties of the Kalinga indicate conclusively an overwhelming preoccupation with spirits of the dead and other malevolent spirits. The spirit helpers of the mediums help to cure when petitioned and sacrifices are offered to them, but they are not benevolent beings.

Thus, the supernaturals, with *Kaboníyan* excepted, must be constantly appeased and compromised. Failure to offer prayers, wine, and sacrificial victims causes them to respond with vengeance, sending illness and death and destroying swiddens and rice fields. Supernaturals are regarded as enemy much in the same manner as nonkin beyond the borders of the regional unit. The difference is that supernaturals are propitiated, but the human enemy, at least in the past, was controlled by defensive warfare or by periodic offensive retaliatory forays. It is significant, however, that intraregional disputes and conflicts suggest the pattern followed with supernaturals. Relatives of an individual who transgressed against another paid wergilds to the latter's relatives and then capped the settlement with a feast, the *palános* or *paínom*. With the cessation of headhunting and warfare, the practice of settling disputes in the home region has been extended to interregional conflicts through the machinery of the peace pact. The feast which terminates the establishment of a pact between two regions or the renewal of such a pact resembles the *palános* and both types of feasts are similar to sacrificial feasts given on the occasion of a curing or funeral ceremony. The guests in the latter feast are invisible members of the spirit world; in the *palános* they are visibly present, the offended kindred; and in the peace pact celebration, they are members of a former hostile region. In all cases, the guests are potentially dangerous and only tactful and generous treatment of them by the hosts will keep them friendly and compromised.

Kalinga hostilities are directed outside the kindred; within this group there is remarkably little conflict. A child is made aware of the large number of relatives as soon as he becomes conscious of his external surroundings. Formal visits such as the *omóy pasíbit, omapó, balón di babát,* and *mamilók* impress upon the child at an early age the host of bilateral relatives who are concerned about his well-being. Virtually every important ritualistic event reinforces this bond so that an individual soon develops a strong loyalty to his group. In the northern Kalinga regions where the kindred is believed to embrace the entire regional population, kindred loyalty binds everyone together.

Kindred relations are marked by considerable freedom of action, with acceptance and tolerance of one another. These characteristics are instilled in a highly permissive childhood training period, but the permissive development goes on relatively unchecked into adulthood. Transgressions occur within the kindred, but these are usually resolved quickly, openly and without leaving deeply rooted grudges. Moreover, since a large segment of an individual's kindred takes the blame for an action, these relatives act as a buffer for him by sharing the unpleasant task of paying fines and otherwise making adjustments. The Kalinga grows into old age, then, with deep loyalties and trust in his kindred. His suspicions and fears are directed instead at the supernatural world and nonkin who are spatially removed. Kindred loyalty and trust, as they operate among the Kalinga, have largely eliminated suspicion and distrust within the group.

No society is entirely free of conflict among closely interacting kin, and the Kalinga are no exception; yet the relations among parents, parents' siblings and their children are remarkably free of friction. The spouses of these relatives are, of course, also included in the kindred (see kinship circle or kindred in Chapter 1).

It is important here to indicate another contributing factor for the rarity of intrakin conflict. Kalinga settlements (except for some of the Southern Kalinga towns) are small and dispersed, and until recently were moved frequently within the region. This type of settlement pattern, which has nevertheless allowed for periodic interaction of kin, undoubtedly fosters greater tension-free relationships among closely related kin.

Kalinga religious values reflect conditions in the Kalinga temporal life in a remarkably accurate fashion. Perhaps all traditional religions of fairly homogenous societies mirror the world of the living in this way. Such key concepts as vengeance, appeasement, and generosity which operate in the everyday life of the Kalinga also characterize the behavior of supernaturals and the latter's relations with mortals. Supernatural spirits like mortals are considered vengeful, inflicting illness and death when not properly honored. Offerings to the spirits may be compared with the payment of fines or wergilds among mortals and thus compromising the injured party. Generosity is demonstrated to spirits by the lavsh feasts prepared for them, which they are believed to share with mortals. Whether the Kalinga believe that spirits can be generous is not apparent, but they obviously hope so. Generosity is a trait they exploit to extreme degrees among themselves, however. It is keynoted in the gracious hospitality extended to visitors and the *palános* feast given to honor them. A related concept, that of indebtedness, is maintained with supernaturals and the living. Prayers and offerings obligate the supernaturals to the living while generous hospitality and gifts bind the living with one another in a mutual system of obligations.

Western and Christian Influences

Western ideas and concepts did not forcibly affect the Kalinga until the closing periods of the last century. During the initial Spanish missionization period in the seventeenth century some of the ancestors of the Kalinga surely received Christian indoctrination in the Cagayan missions, but as refugees they undoubtedly quickly divested themselves of such training. The event that brought about important changes among the Kalinga was the Spanish trail from Abra across the Cordillera Central and thence into the Chico valley. This trail was built in the late nineteenth century to supply the military posts which were established to control the periodic raids of the mountain peoples. Contact with Spanish soldiers was probably infrequent, but the trail opened up opportunities for trade and travel and brought the Kalinga in contact either directly with the Ilocano or with groups like the

Tinguian who were in contact with the Ilocano. The Ilocano language undoubtedly became established as a lingua franca at this time in the mountains and with it, Spanish terms diffused into the Kalinga language and other mountain vernaculars. Notions about Spanish rule and political divisions present among the Kalinga also diffused, and most important of all, the popular tool for interregional understanding and friendship, the peace pact, was born. All of these factors facilitated the dissemination of Western and Christian concepts during the first decade of the American period when roads and trails were constructed throughout the mountains of northern Luzon.

American control brought political divisions modeled on the Spanish colonial pattern, and a representative form of government. The early lieutenant governors working through local leaders, introduced Western notions of law and order and suppressed headhunting and warfare. The latter had already started with the peace pact system, but American endorsement of the system as well as the training of a native constabulary force accelerated the establishment of law and order. Schools were started and training in health and sanitation were begun so that by the end of the second decade of the nineteenth century a fairly effective foundation for an American version of Western civilization had been laid. The number of American or foreign personnel was small; there were probably no more than a half a dozen Americans in governmental service in the Kalinga subprovince up to the outbreak of World War II. At first, lowland Filipinos occupied important subprovincial and municipal posts, but these were slowly replaced by Kalinga. At present, positions in the government and in the schools, except in missionary establishments, are virtually all in the control of the native population.

Since the third decade of the twentieth century, three religious denominations, one Catholic and two Protestant, have served the Kalinga population. The number of actual converts is minimal; the Kalinga have not embraced Christianity in vast numbers. The reason for the few converts is primarily the problem of establishing an effective missionary program in an extremely rugged area where the settlements are reached only by precipitous trails which are almost inaccessible during the rainy season. Missionary personnel is also entirely inadequate in numbers to serve such a mountainous population. Almost the whole of the northern Kalinga area, for example, is served by two Roman Catholic priests resident in Salegseg. One priest, the rector of the mission, administers to the *población* and nearby hamlets, while his assistant serves other hamlets in Salegseg and hamlets in the regions of Poswoy, Ababaan, Daoangan, Balbalan proper, Banao, Mabaca, and Buaya. This is an area of approximately 1000 square miles interlaced with rugged mountain ridges and deep gorges. The hamlets are dispersed in the sides and pockets of steep mountains and the trails leading into them go over rocks which in the rainy season get extremely slippery. In order to get over these trails the priest, like the natives, must take off his shoes to reach the settlements. In addition, the lower elevations of the area are infected with the malarial mosquito. While the disease may now be averted by taking malarial pills at regular intervals, the many demands made on the priest for administering to the sick and the dying and conducting religious services cause him to forget to take the pills regularly. Both priests at Salegseg during the period of my study had contracted malaria early in their missionary work and were often incapacitated by malarial fever.

The priests have trained native catechists for each of the regions of their district who provide instruction in Catholic doctrine in the local hamlets and thus relieve the priests of some of the routine work. Nevertheless, the administration of the sacraments must be given by a priest; hence, there is the need to make periodic visits to the isolated hamlets. When the rector's assistant leaves the mission post for his round of visits, he is gone for two to six weeks before returning to the home mission.

The missionary efforts of both Protestants and Catholics are frustrated by limited personnel and by a rugged, mountainous terrain. Most of the Kalinga converts come from the mission schools where Christian indoctrination is carried on over longer periods of time and under more intensive circumstances. The Kalinga do not object to missionaries and are friendly to all denominations whether Protestant or Catholic. Most Kalinga who profess to be Christians are Roman Catholics. This is because the clergy of this denomination, represented by the Belgian Fathers, have staked out the heart of the Kalinga region for missionary work. Some Kalinga have also become affiliated with the Episcopal mission at Balbalasan and the United Brethren Church at Lubuagan and profess to be members of these denominations. The Philippine Lutheran Mission group began work among the Kalinga in 1960 with a mission station at Basao, Tinglayan municipal district.

Although the number of actual converts to either Catholicism or the Protestant denominations is small, Western and Christian concepts have diffused widely among the Kalinga. The cessation of headhunting and the reorganization of the rituals involving this activity must have been activated by Western contact. Undoubtedly the introduction of firearms and the realization that these new weapons threatened mass slaughter led to the development of the peace pacts. Other changes attributable to Western influences include the omission of many of the ritual steps in the *kontad,* marriage, and death ceremonies. The enthusiastic involvement of the Kalinga in provincial and municipal elections and politics is also indicative of Western influences. The Kalinga at present are active in clubs and committees, organizations which were, perhaps initially triggered by missionaries and early American school teachers. Schooling is highly valued and higher education is a desideratum of almost every Kalinga. Finally, of dubious value but nevertheless stemming from American contact, is the desire for Western products even though they may be inferior to their own natively manufactured items. A particularly glaring example of this is the corrugated tin roofs which are rapidly replacing the old cogongrass roofs. The latter shed rain as effectively and keep the house cooler, but a tin-roofed house marks the residence of an influential and sophisticated man!

4

Warfare and Headhunting

THE REGIONAL CHARACTER of Kalinga population is most pronounced in the rugged mountains of the present municipal districts of Tinglayan, Lubuagan, Tanudan, and Balbalan. Adherence to well-defined territorial regions in these areas is conditioned partly by the presence of well-marked geographical features such as gorges and mountain ridges, but also because of the desire of the local endogamous population for social cohesion. Kalinga regional populations marry with one another, and individuals within a regional unit are closely linked by kinship ties. Formerly each region presented a united opposition to other regions by periodic headhunting forays or by retaliatory attacks to avenge a killing, injury, or other wrong inflicted upon it by another region.

In the foothills and plains of the present Pinokpok and Tabuk municipal districts, Kalinga populations are not restricted to territorial regions as in the more rugged terrain. For about a century and a half, this northeastern area was an unoccupied buffer zone between the aggressively prosletyzing Spanish missionaries and lowland Christian populations on one side and the hostile mountain populations on the other. It was an area which, if settled, might have been preyed upon by either group—by the mountain peoples for heads and by the Christian populations for workers to serve as carriers or in other tasks equally hard and uncompensated. In addition to such dangers, the area was also more heavily infested with the malarial mosquito than either the mountains or the Cagayan Valley. Within the last half-century, with the establishment of peace and some successful results in malarial control, Kalinga populations have begun to move into this formerly unoccupied territory. Some of these migrants remain covered by peace pacts instituted in former home regions, and where new peace pacts have been made, such pacts cover variously a single community and at times, a whole series of settlements; but such pacts do not extend over specifically defined territorial regions as among the Kalinga of the mountainous terrain.

The regional, endogamous character of Kalinga populations in the rugged mountains may also not go back very far into the past since interregional cultural and linguistic differences are not extreme enough to indicate long separation of these units. It is likely that territorial consciousness began as recently as the early decades of the eighteenth century when the first Spanish missions were established in the Cagayan Valley. Historical records indicate that large numbers of former foothill or lowland dwellers fled into the mountains to escape the oppressive activities of Spanish missionaries (Keesing 1962:3, 221–237). While there were undoubtedly already people in the mountains, the refugees swelled the population and presumably closely related kin groups settled together forming the nuclei of the present regional population units. In time, these regional populations developed subcultural characteristics and dialectical differences, but American control at the turn of the twentieth century put an end to further interregional differentiation with the suppression of warfare and headhunting. While some of the early American lieutenant governors of the subprovince actively tried to stop warfare and headhunting, their efforts were not alone responsible for the disappearance of the practice. American control acted rather as a catalyst, bringing about changes which made headhunting unpopular and encouraged interregional mobility. The construction of roads and trails, trade and wage-work opportunities, and the opening up of educational institutions all brought about interregional activity. The instrument which afforded interregional travel with guarantee of personal safety was the peace pact institution, in the main a Kalinga invention. This device will be described in some detail in the next chapter, but to understand the Kalinga peace pact system it is important first to characterize Kalinga warfare and headhunting activities as they are remembered by older Kalinga who were active participants.

Warfare

The Kalinga occasionally participated in retaliatory and defensive group skirmishes distinguished from headhunting, but large-scale warfare was unknown. Thus, an alternative method for maintaining territorial boundaries employed by modern nations existed only in embryonic form among the Kalinga. Of the two devices, headhunting is to be preferred from the standpoint of the loss of lives and the destruction of property. Warfare, or battle (*baloknit,* Lubuagan; *botad,* Mabaca) is distinguished terminologically from headhunting (*kilib,* Lubuagan; *kayaw,* Poswoy).

Headhunting involved a small party of men, indeed often a lone warrior. Kalinga warfare or battle on the other hand includes all of a region's available manpower pitted against another such group from an enemy region. Battle is triggered off by some insult, injury, or perhaps a series of killings emanating from another region. Encounters of this kind are always announced; the challengers move up to the regional boundary and from a hill or slope overlooking one of the settlements, shout a challenge. The shouting amounts to a declaration of war; the enemy, having been warned, assembles its warriors along the boundary line. The groups facing each other taunt and insult each other, and hurl rocks; then with spears drawn and shields ready to fend off the opponents' spear thrusts, they begin to move closer. When the group is within spear-throwing range, the real battle gets under way. The challenged group has the option to make peace by agreeing to pay indemnities or make other reparations. However, since a life taken can only be satisfied by substituting another life, a group which has been challenged to war over a killing or a series of killings usually decides to fight it out. Such pitched battles could take a large number of lives if fought to the last man, but Kalinga usually stop after a few men from each side have been mortally wounded and others injured. The side which has fared worst in the encounter initiates the truce, its leaders calling attention to the larger number they have suffered in dead or injured or both. A peace is then effected, indemnities and reparations being made and the affair ended by drinking and feasting. The establishment of peace following a battle was probably the predecessor of modern Kalinga peace pacts. Modern firearms more than any other cause have brought down the incidence of interregional warfare. This type of warfare portends grave consequences and the Kalinga were ready to recognize it. The birth of the peace pact institution may thus be understood as a substitute for Kalinga-type warfare when mass-destruction weapons were introduced. Perhaps to a lesser extent, the peace pact discouraged headhunting or homicide, which still occurs even though the peace pacts also specifically prohibit it.

Peace pact celebrations and interregional visiting, which invariably involve excessive drinking, trigger habitual Kalinga boasting and taunting patterns which fan the flames of old feuds and often lead to the rupture of peace pact alliances. Individuals hesitate to take private vengeance and the offended region may decide to act as a unit by challenging the offending region to war. The affair may not go beyond simply a rattling of headaxes, spears, and shields, but at least pride has been assuaged. And if there is a battle with some lives lost and others injured, it is unlikely that individuals will be sought out to be jailed, for in such encounters the whole regional population is involved. If the Philippine constabulary comes to investigate, regional populations give confusing and misleading information, thus protecting the identity of leaders, and usually no arrests are made. Thus, the threat of interregional warfare is still present and occasionally flares up in temporary scuffles. While the possession of modern weapons by mountain natives is prohibited by Philippine law, many have acquired rifles and pistols during World War II or illegally through trade with lowlanders. And although rifles are used mainly for hunting, the Kalinga are not adverse to using them occasionally in homicide. Recently there were two aborted warfare encounters in the regions of Mabongtot-Mangali and Tinglayan-Sumadel; each group possessed firearms and was prepared to use them. Peace pact holders intervened and averted war, but it was not so much the statesmenship of the pact holders that brought about a rather uneasy peace as the prospect of a bloody, annihilating battle with modern weapons.

Headhunting

Head-taking involved small groups of warriors who had to sneak stealthily into an enemy region, strike suddenly and then flee as soon as an alarm was sounded. Such techniques do not take a large toll of lives on either side and there is no

An elderly Kalinga from the Bugnay-Butbut region (southern Kalinga). Occassional outbreaks of feuds prompt Kalinga men to travel with spears and headaxes. The village of Bugnay and rice terraces are in the background.

destruction of the enemy's land, crops, or possessions. It was not possible to determine the number of heads lost by a regional group to the enemy during the course of a year. Old men who had a reputation for being headhunters boasted of taking ten or more enemy heads, but when asked about the number lost to their own regional population, their estimates became highly conservative. In Bolo in the region of Salegseg, an old warrior considered a half-dozen heads lost to the enemy during the course of a year a reasonable estimate at the height of the head-taking period in his boyhood. He was quick to add, however, that enemy regions lost considerably more, a remark that can probably be discounted as boasting.

Former headhunters report that headhunting activities rarely disrupted routine farming and household activities for long periods. Headhunters did not attack a village unless it was completely unattended; they sought their prey in lone workers in the swiddens or rice fields or on the trail. The victims of the headhunter were disproportionately high in old, infirm men and women. Women from middle age down and children away from home were always in the company of a few men in their prime, but old men and women in their crass independence usually went about alone, refusing the protection offered them by young men. A headhunter achieved distinction regardless of how or whom he killed and beheaded, and the boasting recitals frequently mention old men and women as victims.

Headhunting also served another important function—that of maintaining territorial space. Vayda (1961) points out that the psychological and group-cohesion factors have generally received greater emphasis than ecological factors to explain headhunting and primitive warfare and argues that the latter may be of greater importance. Among the Kalinga, the maintenance of regional boundaries is certainly a by-product of the headhunting complex even though the people themselves cannot explicitly provide such a reason. The Kalinga do not, however, regard the land base itself as in need of defense. There is no competition for swidden land, and among the Northern Kalinga at least, encroachers on irrigated rice fields are not a pressing problem or one of concern, and we believe they were even less so in the past when regional populations were smaller. Thus, the constant fear of enemy headhunters among the Kalinga in the past does not appear to arise out of strictly ecological, economic, or political concerns, but because of personal physical safety. And naturally enough this is the reason given for the defensive measures the Kalinga take and not fear of territorial conquest. Nevertheless, it is clear that the headhunting complex has kept regional boundaries intact.

The ritual activities involving headhunting were as elaborate as those associated with the life cycle and agriculture. In recent years, with the diffusion of Western technology and ideas, virtually all of the rituals connected with headhunting have lapsed or have been reinterpreted. Headhunting or head-taking has occurred only sporadically in recent years, but private vengeance involving either killings or woundings still erupts periodically. The following description of former headhunting and ritual practices is from information obtained from old men who had either participated in the activity as young men or were in their boyhood when headhunting was a live activity. While the version given here comes from the region of Poswoy, northern Kalinga, a check of the data with informants from other regions of northern Kalinga and Lubuagan indicates that practices were similar in these two areas of the present Kalinga subprovince.

As with all important undertakings, the careful observation of omens was important before invading an enemy region for heads. The warriors armed with spears, headaxes, and shields stole into enemy territory, carefully avoiding pitfalls, traps, and warning devices formerly set up by all villages for protection. Open encounter with the enemy was avoided if possible. If a lone man, child, or woman, no matter of what age, could be located, the war party considered itself fortunate. The warriors swooped down on the defenseless victim and quickly severed the head, or if the cries of the victim drew pursuers before the head could be taken, only the hand or fingers might be taken. The invaders retreated, with the enemy usually in hot pursuit at their heels. A pursuing party rarely followed an invading group into the latter's region. When a headhunting party was out, its regional members kept watch for its return, and pursuers would be at distinct disadvantage in a clash between the two groups. Moreover, villages were formerly stockaded and short bamboo sticks with sharpened points were planted along the trails approaching a village to impede rapid travel. Along some of the trails were deadfalls, in the form of an overhanging or leaning, heavy log to be tripped by a string strung across the trail, which would kill a stranger or warn the village of his approach. Some villages also dug pits on the trails. These pits contained sharpened bamboos at the bottom and were ready to catch and maim or kill the unwary stranger. Only the members of the region knew the location of such traps and warning devices. It was thus hazardous for a pursuing enemy group to follow a party of headhunters all the way home. A small headhunting party cautiously entering an enemy region was usually successful in avoiding the traps set by the enemy, but a pursuing party was at a disadvantage because its enemy was prepared to meet it. Moreover, the fleeing party often led pursuers purposely into the traps and thus added to the danger of pursuit.

A returning headhunting party which was successful in its invasion of an enemy region shouted a series of piercing cries about a half a mile from the first town or hamlet of its home region. These cries were answered by the *ayaya* call of the women, an eerie staccato cry made by quick movements of the tongue against the upper teeth. This peculiar call was made only when a victorious headhunting party was returning to its home region. The first cries alerted nearby villages, and women in these villages immediately took up the cry and disseminated the news throughout the region.

The returning headhunters proceeded to the village from which the leader had come or from which most of the party had been drawn. Here excitement and shouts of joy greeted the warriors, and the *potol,* or evidence of the kill, was examined. Preparations for the rituals and festivities which were part of the occasion also began at once. One end of a bamboo stalk about 6 to 10 feet in length and about 3 inches in diameter was fashioned into a basket by stripping the sides. The bamboo stalk called *sakólang* was then taken to the outskirts of the village and planted near the sacred shrine, the *podayán.* The basket-like recepticle was lined with hibiscus flowers and the *potol* (head or heads, hands or fingers) placed inside. While this was going on, relatives of the warriors set out jars of wine, and others tended to the butchering of pigs and the preparation of food. The medium and her helpers meanwhile performed the *sagáng* ceremony. The chants of this headhunting ceremony were no longer remembered by my informants, but the medium was said to petition *sangásang,* the guardian of the village, to bestow long life on the warriors. During the ceremony, she removed the *potol* from the *sakó-lang* and placed it on top of the sacred rocks (*bayóg*) which forms part of the sacred shrine. Later, upon completing her chants in the shrine, the medium returned the *potol* to the *sakólang* where it remained during the rest of the festivities, which went on for two days.

In the frenzied excitement of the initial meeting of regional members and the returning warriors, the skullcap might be removed from severed heads and some of the brains and wine mixed together. This mixture was then drunk by the warriors to make them courageous and successful warriors (Worcester 1912). The severed heads, hands, or fingers remained in the *sakólang* during the festivities, however, and later the *potol* was boiled and the bones and broken bits of the skull passed around to the participant warriors as trophies. Most prized was the lower jaw which served as the handle of the chief musical instrument of the Kalinga, the Chinese gong or *ganza*. Having participated in a headhunting expedition also entitled a warrior to a tattoo, *dakag*. A man need not have killed an enemy; merely having been present with a party that had killed gave him the right to be tattooed. Most Kalinga men who now have tattoos received them as the result of having killed Japanese soldiers during the closing periods of World War II. Women were reported to have the privilege of being tatooed whenever any male relative had received his tattoo. Since all regional members are considered related, a woman is always able to find some tattooed male relative who gives her the right to be tattooed.

From the reports of informants, a headhunting feast appears to resemble a modern peace pact celebration in broad outline, although the latter never reaches the frenzied and orgiastic proportions of the headhunting rites (see Chapter 5). Men and women sat or squatted about a central area where varied types of activities were performed. Most common on the program was a series of dances. The dances were periodically interrupted by the singing of special war songs. Occasionally too, men who had participated in headhunting expeditions gave a pantomimic demonstration of how they had killed and severed heads. The warriors reenacted the headhunting scene by leaping and prancing around, brandishing spears, shields, and headaxes as if they were fighting with an enemy warrior. As the pitch of excitement increased and the large quantities of wine they had drunk began to take effect, old headhunting veterans moved into the circle to relate their war exploits (*palpaliwat, pokaw*). These were related in a stylized chant while the narrator postured grotesquely. Words were improvised, but how carefully and appropriately a warrior chose his words and how cleverly he rhymed them marked him as a master of the art. Some of the old headhunters goaded the young men to hunt for heads and spoke of those who did not dare to engage in the practice as despicable weaklings.

The reasons for and functions of headhunting among the mountain people of northern Luzon have been generally attributed to religious factors, most specifically to fertility concepts (Worcester 1912:875; Folkmar 1906; Barton 1949:236). With the Kalinga at least, fertility concepts involving the miraculous increase of crops and human life as an associated aspect of headhunting appear to be absent, except that there is widespread belief that the taking of the life of an enemy may cure childlessness in one's wife or female relative. Barrenness may be dispelled by bringing death to a nonregional member by any method, however, not necessarily by the expediency of headhunting. The belief is the basis for the admonition given to all travelers to refuse food offered by a childless woman lest the unwary traveler be poisoned to help rid the woman of her barrenness. The association of headhunting practices with agricultural activities was denied by my informants and no ritual activities were reported to have been associated with rice fields or swiddens either before or following a headhunting expedition. The reasons given for participating in a headhunting venture were the following: (1) to retaliate an attack by enemy headhunters; (2) to "even the score" when a man has lost a close relative either by natural death or as the result of an accident; (3) to gain prestige and renown (see Chapter 3).

The final reason given above was the one most often cited by the Kalinga themselves for the existence of headhunting. The respect and esteem in which the headhunter is held even at present confirms these assertions, and the behavior formerly associated with headhunting activities further underscores the prestige factor. Thus, successful headhunters were welcomed upon their return from a headhunting expedition with an elaborate celebration, and their headhunting achievements were recounted at other subsequent festivities. The prestige rewards of headhunting undoubtedly kept the practice alive during the Spanish period despite the efforts of civil and religious authorities to put an end to it. These valued prestige by-products of headhunting also brought about the temporary revival of the practice during the general unrest following the overthrow of Spanish rule at the turn of the century and again at the end of the Japanese occupation period in 1944-1945. Indeed, headhunting still occurs occasionally in remote areas, as it did briefly in the spring of 1960 in the Natonin area of eastern Kalinga. So ingrained is the esteem accorded a headhunter that the glorification of older men who have taken heads has been made a part of the program celebrating interregional peace pacts at present. These performances are given as the final act of the peace pact celebration. On this occasion, men who have killed or taken heads in the past boast proudly of their exploits (see Chapter 5).

A Kalinga man formerly sought status by an illustrious headhunting record, and it was indeed about the only avenue open to him for distinction. This is particularly true in the north where cultivation of dry rice did not permit the accumulation of wealth, which was an alternative to power and influence among the ethnic groups in the south. Even among the Kalinga of Lubuagan, techniques of irrigated rice farming had diffused quite early, so that it was possible to amass wealth in rice fields. Elsewhere, we have noted the beginnings of important descent groups in Lubuagan and the rise of aristocratic families, or *kadangyan,* which were distinguished from others because of greater wealth. Among both the Southern and Northern Kalinga, status was achieved primarily by personal efforts, but the road to power and influence was easier in Lubuagan, for example, to a man who already belonged to a highly ranked family. Among the Northern Kalinga, class distinctions were apparently nonexistent in the past, and even at present they are lightly drawn. But a brave, even ruthless man could take heads, kill, and wound and eventually work up the status ladder. A record of many killings made such a man feared and respected and earned him the title of *mangol,* or brave warrior. People were afraid of such men, but they were also proud to be identified with them, for a regional population enjoyed high status and security if it could count among its members men of *mangol* rank. Besides a distinguished headhunting record, a man enjoyed status if he could increase his family's heirloom collection of Chinese jars, plates, and beads. In order to accumulate these possessions in large numbers, it was almost essential to have *mangol* status, for such men could purchase such precious items from others for lesser amounts than others might be expected to pay simply because they were powerful and feared. Also, since such men had avenged again and again the losses and injuries suffered by coregionists, the latter felt indebted to these distinguished warriors and usually gave them what they asked. Early observers among the Kalinga report of such men as highly feared and respected individuals. An account of a journey into the northern Kalinga country by Worcester in 1905 describes an encounter with headhunting Kalinga. Worcester credits a man of *mangol* status by the name of Bakidan for saving the lives of his party. We quote a few excerpts from Worcester's interesting account (Worcester and Hayden 1930:432–433):

> It was fortunate indeed for us that we made friends with Bakidan. On the following day we continued our journey down the valley. Our baggage was carried by women, children and a few old and more or less decrepit warriors who obviously felt deeply insulted at being required to render such a menial service, and were decidedly resentful toward Bakidan for having ordered them to do it.
> Before we started Bakidan warned us that the Kalingas were queer people, and in consequence it would be well for us very quietly to go around certain of their settlements. Others we would visit. Their inhabitants would be sure to invite us to stay and enjoy their hospitality. He would second every such invitation. We were to pay no attention to his words, but were to note whether or not he sat down. If he did, we might accept the invitation. Otherwise we must plead an urgent engagement farther down the valley and move on.
> Things came out exactly as he had foretold. In several villages we heard noises decidedly suggestive of head-*cañaos* [head feasts], and discreetly circled these places. We declined all invitations seconded by Bakidan when he did not seat himself, and rested comfortably for a time in several villages where he did. Toward noon we walked straight into an ambush laid for us in the *runo* grass, discovering it only when Bakidan began to deliver a forceful oration in which he set forth the fact that he had a right to stroll down his own valley with a party of friends without being annoyed by having his fellow tribesmen hide beside the trail and prepare to throw lances.
> Bakidan who was himself a famous warrior, told these men that they might kill us if they saw fit to do so, but must kill him first. Apparently, rather ashamed of themselves, they came out on to the trail and slunk off to their town. Bakidan,

greatly disgusted, suggested that we follow them and lunch in their village, just to show that we were not afraid of them, and we did this . . .

The people of his village received us in a most friendly spirit, and after attending a bit of a *cañao* [feast] organized in our honour, and doing our best to entertain the crowd with a few simple experiments in physics, and some sleight-of-hand tricks, we retired, as we supposed, for a peaceful night's rest. No such good fortune awaited us. We were aroused in the middle of the night by a fearful din only to find our hut surrounded by a great circle of armed men. The people who had attempted to ambush us earlier in the day had repented of their action in letting us pass through unharmed, had gathered a strong force of fighting men, had surrounded our house and were now vociferously demanding to be allowed to take our heads . . . . Bakidan was our only advocate. He still insisted that any one who wished to kill us must kill him first. His reputation stood him in good stead, and no one tackled the job.

While a leader like Bakidan instills fear among all who know his reputation, any group is also afraid of the retaliation from a leader's kindred should harm come to him. It is thus not only the *mangol* who is feared but all of his relatives who are indebted to him in many different ways. It is instructive to sketch briefly the development of a *mangol* to see how he achieves power and influence.

An ambitious young man accompanied experienced warriors on his first headhunting expedition. In his first encounter with the enemy, he guarded against panic, watched the behavior of seasoned headhunters and learned to be calm and collected. He also carefully observed the proper wielding of the spear, headaxe, and shield. If his party took a head in his first headhunting venture, even if he himself did not take part in the kill, he was entitled to his tattoo. In later headhunting trips, he would venture more boldly and sooner or later, if he was lucky, he too would kill. As he matured, learned his art to greater perfection, and fortune permitting, he added to his victims. More and more, the regional population became aware of the young man and watched him in headhunting feasts as he performed pantomimic reenactments of headhunting feats and boasted of the numbers he had slain. Feeling his power, he might even kill within his region to avenge a killing or wounding even though such a case might have been resolved amicably among people who knew each other and whose kindreds overlap. Disdainfully, in regional festivals, he taunted his coregionists for not matching his headhunting record and as he began to speak up in the informal councils, coregionists began to consult him in their troubles and ask him to settle disputes. Thus he became an "arbiter" as well. His home became a gathering place for relatives and friends, and as a man of influence in keeping with Kalinga values, he was hospitable and generous, frequently holding a *paínom* or *palános* (a feast to entertain friends). As a rising *mangol,* he had no trouble acquiring one or more *dagdagas* (mistresses) who helped elevate his prestige. He also began to add to his heirloom possessions, using his power and influence to secure these items. At this point, he had arrived at the pinnacle of Kalinga success as it was reckoned in headhunting days some sixty or seventy years ago.

It is essential to emphasize that *mangol* status was achieved and could not be passed on to family or relatives. While a *mangol* was alive, all those associated with him enjoyed the respect and deference shown him, but upon his death, people turned to other powerful and influential men. The important ingredient in *mangol* status was a distinguished headhunting and homicide record. The only tangible property which came down to a *mangol*'s relatives was the heirloom possessions he had acquired, but these were usually quickly dissipated by the surviving kin to curry the favor of other men of *mangol* rank. The sons of a *mangol* were no better equipped than others in the region to achieve the rank of a courageous warrior, for bravery, headhunting skills, and a distinguished war record could not be inherited.

With the disappearance of headhunting, the avenue to power and influence has been rechanneled and now men may achieve status by wealth and political activity. A man may also derive some degree of importance and influence by positions achieved by specialized training and schooling, such as that of a municipal clerk or a schoolteacher. Nevertheless, the rewards to be derived from headhunting have not altogether disappeared. There are sporadic occurrences of headhunting and at the end of the Japanese occupation when Japanese soldiers could be hunted with impunity, young men had a heyday rooting out Japanese soldiers from hiding places, luring them into homes with promise of food, and then falling upon them and hacking up their bodies. Most of the skull fragments and jaw bones possessed by the Kalinga at present come from this temporary resurgence of headhunting. Thus, the attraction of headhunting or head-taking has not disappeared; it is only that the penalty for homicide is high and the practice is inconvenient and impractical when wage work, schooling, and other recent changes make traveling through former enemy regions imperative. To some extent, private vengeance through killing or woundings, whether within the region or without, satisfies the old headhunting craze. But vengeance is also prompted by a desire to uphold kinship pride, and some individuals engage in it against their wills to satisfy the constant urging of relatives to avenge when one of their members has been killed or injured. While wergilds are usually paid in these cases, the kinship group operating in an older set of values is rarely satisfied unless blood is drawn. Minor cases of woundings or injuries are sometimes resolved by token woundings where the individual who committed the act, whether intentional or not, submits himself (or provides a substitute) to be wounded or injured in the same manner and in the same place. Yet there are individuals who are feared, distrusted, and admired because they will not let a killing or injury be resolved other than by vengeance. This is particularly true of individuals in the Lubuagan region and other densely populated regions in the south which usually resolve killings and woundings by counterkillings or which demand enormous wergild payments with the threat of vengeance; even when wergilds are paid, such regional populations may not always refrain from retaliation. Barton (1949:231–232) provides numerous examples of killings and woundings for which wergild payments were accepted and the settlement thus made violated by retaliation. Desire to uphold kinship pride may be involved in cases of retaliation even when wergilds are accepted, but prestige factors also motivate personal avengers.

The Kalinga, as with most people in any society, are not introspective about their culture; they do not attempt to seek other than obvious reasons for a custom. It is apparent, however, that headhunting among the Kalinga served other purposes besides vengeance, retaliation, and prestige. The practice undoubtedly provided the psychological need to release aggression and also served to foster and maintain regional solidarity. Older informants speak with nostalgia about the pleasurable excitement in preparing for and setting out on a headhunting raid, shared in no less intensity by kinfolk and neighbors at home. Headhunting forays of the enemy might even have been welcomed as a break to long, tedious hours of work in the fields and the routine performance of daily tasks. An enemy raid provided diversion as well as danger; it was a pleasurable tingling of excitement for everybody and there was always the possibility for men to kill or wound and thus achieve or add to their laurels.

While headhunting has virtually disappeared, private revenge in the form of killings and woundings is common. From reports received during the field research period, it is no exaggeration to say that in each region, two to three killings and some dozen woundings annually can be attributed to the vengeance motive. Such acts of vengeance are always explained as "payments" for previous killings or woundings of a member or members of the avenger's kinship group. These "payments" may be for "debts" of long standing between two kindreds or they may be vengeance for a killing or injury which took place moments before.

Even minor injuries, cuts, or wounds, if inflicted by another, must be settled to the satisfaction of the injured party's kindred. Whether the injury was intentionally or accidentally inflicted is of little importance; all injuries caused by the instrumentality of another person must be settled or explained. If the injury was caused by a member of the same kindred, an explanation of the facts to an older male kin of both individuals involved is the initial step. The male relative then talks to the immediate families of the two people involved and settles the problem amicably by providing a token gift from the family of the individual responsible for the act to the family of the injured party. Among the Northern Kalinga, intraregional troubles are usually handled in the same manner as injuries or disputes that arise between two immediate families of the same kindred. This is because the whole regional unit is conceived to be a single kindred. When populations are dense and there are many overlapping kindreds, as in the region of Lubuagan and other regions in the south, intraregional difficulties are often resolved by resort to vengeance. In all intraregional troubles, however, the immediate move of regional leaders is to explore the possibility of settling the problem peaceably and quietly. This ideal does not always succeed, however, for hotheaded individuals take up a bolo (the Philippine long knife similar to the Mexican machete), headaxe, or spear and strike a member of the offending party's kindred before an investigation and settlement is made. The role of the regional leader is important in settling intraregional disputes and beginning in the latter part of the nineteenth century to the present, in interregional problems as well, via the peace pact institution. Before the spread of the peace pacts, however, interregional troubles could be satisfied only by resorting to headhunting practises. The existence of a peace pact between two regions does not, of course, preclude that troubles or disputes will be resolved peaceably. When there is trouble between two regions, pact-holders try to get together immediately to settle the problem before individuals from the injured party's region take vengeance and compound the difficulties. Travel outside the region is postponed or reduced strictly in order to avoid the possibility of individuals from the two regions encountering one another. But meetings do occur and vengeance is often taken despite efforts to prevent it. On my initial trip to the Northern Kalinga country, my hosts in Lubuagan insisted that I take as a guide a youth of the extended family. Since Lubuagan had peace pacts with Salegseg and Mabaca where I was bound, it was felt that the youth was perfectly safe. On the public Dangwa transportation bus or truck, we learned that two school boys, one from Salegseg and the other from Lubuagan, had had a fist fight. One of the boys had received a bloody nose. The information was confused; no one knew which one of the boys had started the fight or which one had gotten the worst of the encounter, but my young companion was panic stricken. He was safe on the truck, for by a kind of tacit agreement among the mountain tribes, no one is permitted to resort to vengeance while riding a public conveyance. My companion was afraid, however, of what might happen to him when we arrived at the end of the truck route in Salegseg. I suggested that he ride back to Lubuagan on the truck, but he had, of course, to spend part of an afternoon and night in Salegseg, for the truck did not return to Lubuagan until the following day. Besides, he felt that he ought to fulfill his obligation of being my companion and carrier for another long day of hiking over a tortuous trail to Mabaca still ahead of us. But his fears suddenly disappeared at Salegseg when more accurate news was received and it was learned that the Salegseg boy had started the fight and that the Lubuagan boy had gotten the worst of it. It was the Salegseg population which would now be afraid and apprehensive until satisfactory settlement could be made between the two regions. Retaliation was most unlikely from my companion, who was timid by temperament and among strangers; he was happy to let someone else even the score.

Headhunting and private revenge can resolve conflicts without annihilating regional populations. This type of homicide undoubtedly represents a very early type of device to settle disputes between kinship units. The principle of collective responsibility protected the anonymity of the headhunter or private avenger. The latter, in Kalinga belief, was performing a service for his kindred and region. While vengeance from the enemy region was almost sure to come, the successful avenger himself was no more nor no less in danger of his life than anyone else in his region. At present, as headhunting has been legally outlawed and also prohibited by the peace pact, an instance of homicide demands finding the actual killer. Since the kind of anonymity that formerly protected the headhunter and avenger has been removed, individuals are not so ready to seek private vengeance. Further, modern conditions have devalued the prestige factor in headhunting and it is now possible to achieve distinction by ways other than killing. Yet feuds between regions are deeply rooted and not easily forgotten.

The vengeance pattern places workers and students in locations away from their home regions in a difficult position. News of troubles which involve two different regions travels to individuals of these regions living far away who may be

A woman peace pact holder from the Poswoy region (northern Kalinga). Note the tatoo on her arm.

friends. The one whose regional member was killed or wounded by a member of his friend's kindred is put into the awkward and unpleasant position of having to kill or wound his friend in order to live up to kinship expectations. The vengeance system thus continues the distrust and fear of one another among the Kalinga of different regions who are working or pursuing an education together. Many Kalinga today would like to place friendship ties above kinship responsibilities, but an individual can never be completely certain of the reaction of a friend when a member of his own kinship group has wronged a member of his friend's kindred. The kinship tie is still the most important bond of the Kalinga and indeed generally among Filipinos. It is undoubtedly the factor which explains the instability of political parties and the paucity and ineffectiveness of extrakinship institutions throughout the Philippines (compare Lande 1958:174–207).

5

The Peace Pact Institution

THE KALINGA PEACE PACT INSTITUTION (*bodong*) is obviously a response to recent historical developments. The former regional isolationism of the Kalinga was broken by Western cultural penetration, particularly by creating opportunities for trade and travel. The earliest dates on which peace pacts were actually established occur around the turn of the century. The beginning of such pacts was probably initiated even earlier, possibly with the establishment of a Spanish military "road" or trail from Abra over the Cordillera Central into the Saltan and Chico valleys during the latter part of the nineteenth century. As interregional travel and trade became more common during the first and second decades of the twentieth century, the number of peace pacts increased. Indeed, new pacts are still being made as travel into relatively more isolated areas opens up.

Given the traditional animosity between regions, the headhunting practices, and the vengeance system, measures to safeguard the interregional traveler had to be taken when extensive travel became feasible. The Kalinga's answer to this problem was the peace pact which is simply a more formal adjudication system already employed to deal with intraregional, intrakindred problems. The peace pact system is, therefore, not something revolutionarily new. The Kalinga, like other mountain peoples of northern Luzon, have a complex legal system, obviously very old, to handle local regional problems. This body of procedures was simply incorporated into the peace pact system and now these laws are called upon to resolve interregional problems as well. The peace pact meetings or celebrations, for example, resemble the lounging sessions of regional leaders during a *kontad*, wedding, or funeral ceremony. Peace pact meetings give an opportunity for local leaders to exhibit their oratorical skill before a wider audience and to be instrumental in settling the problems of a larger population.

The peace pact system may have been suggested by the trading partnerships widespread throughout the Philippines and in Borneo as reported by Barton (1949:144–145), but it is primarily a response to changes brought about by Western contact and influence and not simply a device indicative of the arrival of the

Kalinga at a point in social evolution where "territorial units are dominating the kinship groups" (Barton 1949:137). Particular historical, economic, ecological, or other circumstances must be sought to explain the change from one type of social organization into another. It is no accident, therefore, that the peace pact system arose among the Kalinga who were in an area where Western influences first penetrated the restricted and regionally bounded mountain populations. Peace pacts are most numerous among the Kalinga of the Chico and Saltan River valleys, and the pacts between the Kalinga and Tinguian of Abra are more complex than with any other non-Kalinga people. This is, of course, precisely the area through which ran the Spanish trail that opened up travel and trade opportunities into one of the most isolated areas of northern Luzon.

We have considerable variation in the practices of the Kalinga cultural and social subsystems already described. This variation is observable not only between the Northern and Southern Kalinga, but also from region to region within the subcultural divisions of the Kalinga subprovince. The development of regional autonomy and the animosity between regions have undoubtedly produced these differences. The peace pact institution, since it is an interregional peace mechanism, attempts to ameliorate rather than intensify differences. Its avowed purpose is to find solutions to interregional troubles by ways other than those traditionally employed in a blood-feud system.

Within each region, fairly satisfactory and consistent methods of arbitration and compromise by appeal to an intricate body of custom laws have long existed. The arbiter in the home region was the successful headhunter, acknowledged as a leader because he was feared and respected. In the south, family connection and property have also been associated with the role of the arbiter, but the additional attributes of a brave warrior were also requisite. In recent years, as headhunting became illegal and inconvenient or impractical, the tendency has been everywhere to stress wealth, an aggressive personality, and forceful speech habits as traits of the arbiter. The former characteristics have not completely disappeared; it is still considered proper, if the situation warrants it, for a regional leader to kill an offender of custom law (or a member of his kindred) who refused to abide by the decisions mutually agreed upon by a group of regional leaders. These arbiters do not meet as a formal body, but an offense or crime is discussed informally in the frequent festivals or ceremonial occasions where regional leaders are wont to discuss the affairs of the region. Through long discussion a kind of unanimous decision about a matter is reached and one of the arbiters makes the pronouncement on the offender's family.

The regional pattern of adjudicating wrongs sketched above has been transferred virtually intact to the peace pact system. In broad outline, Kalinga regional adjudication systems are much the same, but there are differences among the laws from region to region which become greater with distance. These differences bring about problems to the interregional leaders, who must work them out into a coherent and mutually agreed upon set of provisions (the *pagta*) which is the central feature of the peace pact. But decisions are reached as evidenced by the expansion of the peace pact system in recent years.

A peace pact is initiated by two individuals from different regions and each one of the individuals holds the peace pact for his particular kinship group, although its provisions are binding on the whole region. The procedure in instituting a peace pact can be conveniently illustrated by a hypothetical case. In this fictitious account I have attempted to reproduce as faithfully as possible the social environment and emotional atmosphere in which a peace pact is born, and have followed its development step by step to the ratification of the pact and the celebration following. I have introduced a number of incidents which frequently occur in specific cases in the establishment of a pact between two regions, but it is unlikely that all of the incidents presented here will ever occur in any one of them.

Let us suppose that Juanito from region A has met Emilio from region B in Lubuagan where both have come to trade. No peace pact exists between regions A and B. Let us suppose, also, that the Lubuagan pact-holder for region A also holds the one for region B; thus he is hosting both Juanito and Emilio. Commonly a pact-holder has two pacts, and he may even have as many as four, although beyond this number it is considered too much of a hardship for any one person.

In our hypothetical case, there are a number of visitors from regions A and B, and so the Lubuagan peace pact holder decides to give a *palános* (or *paínom*), a friendship feast, to honor his guests, to display his generosity, and to uphold his prestige. A *palános* is open to all of a host's kindred and many of these come, as well as some of the prominent men of the region who have a standing invitation to all such feasts. Pigs are butchered and wine flows freely. Juanito and Emilio find themselves squatting next to each other at meal time and become acquainted. Later they come together again over cups of wine and begin to exchange information about the character of one another's region. Both know, of course, that no peace pact exists between their regions, for all adult Kalinga, especially traders and travelers, know all the peace pacts held by their region. They are also aware of the status of these pacts, that is, whether they have been broken, reinstituted or are in the process of being reestablished. This information is vital, for one's life is in danger should he be in a region with which his own region has no pact or in a region which has just broken its peace pact with his own.

Let us suppose that a peace pact has never been instituted between A and B. This would not be the case today if both regions are in the Kalinga subprovince, for these regions all have or have had peace pacts with one another for many years, although new ones are still being made outside of the subprovince of Kalinga. But if we assume that this is a new pact, we can present all of the important steps that lead to a formally instituted pact between the two regions.

As the wine brings about good feeling between Juanito and Emilio, they begin to discuss trade opportunities. Juanito learns that Chinese beads and jars bring handsome prices in region B, and Emilio is amazed at how cheaply carabaos may be bought in region A. The idea of a peace pact with themselves as pact-holders occurs to them at once, and in the morning before leaving, they decide to talk over the matter with their respective regional leaders as soon as they return home.

At home, Juanito meets with partial disappointment for the *lakays* or regional leaders do not consider him forceful enough to be a pact-holder. The *lakays* had found an opportunity to discuss the matter of a peace pact between the two regions at a *koliás* for old Capitán X who had died a year previously (see description of *koliás*, Chapter 2). The *koliás* drew all the important regional leaders together, for Capitán X had been a *mangol* and an outstanding arbiter. The *lakays,* as they lounged around a fire outside the former dwelling of Capitán

X, had discussed the matter far into the night and had reached a decision only in the evening of the second day. They reviewed all of the past grievances between region A and B and were particularly incensed over the killing of Capitán Y by a man from region B in 1930 at Lubuagan. Lubuagan had met its peace pact obligations to region A by immediately bringing the body of Capitán Y to his family in region A and sending as well a pig for the funeral feast. Lubuagan, too, had at once sent a stern warning to region B's peace pact holder for Lubuagan, indicating that the peace pact between Lubuagan and region B was in serious danger of rupture for a man with whom Lubuagan had a peace pact had been killed on Lubuagan soil. It is said that region B made an immediate and handsome restitution to Lubuagan, but ignored region A. Since no peace pact existed between A and B, the only recourse would have been a counterkilling by region B. Indeed several attempts had been made and a youth from region A almost succeeded in 1950 of evening the score. The youth had knifed an old woman from region B in the market at Baguio. The woman had almost died, but since she lived, the old score remained unsettled. The youth was unfortunately caught in the act and is still serving a sentence for attempted homicide.

So the *lakayas* of region A were very much concerned that a forceful man who would have the fear and respect of both regions should hold the pact for region B. The pact-holder must, of course, come from Juanito's descent group (see Chapter 1) for Juanito had initiated the matter. In their deliberations the regional leaders finally decided that Juanito's first cousin, Balniwit, a son of Juanito's mother's sister had the requisite courage. "For, did he not immediately avenge his first cousin Pedro's spear wound in the thigh inflicted by a man from region X by cutting a gash in the arm of a youth from region X he had met in Tabuk?" He was a man who acted quickly and fearlessly. Besides, he was already a pact-holder for region Y, a tough region which always insisted on a heavy *dosa* (wergild) from other regions, but Balniwit was feared and respected there and region Y did not try to take any advantage of region A.

The next day, Balniwit's spear was dispatched to Emilio in region B. The spear was accepted by Emilio himself; apparently he had been found to possess the requisite characteristics of a pact-holder by his own regional leaders. In turn, Emilio sent his spear to Balniwit and so the preliminary stage, a period of truce called *sipat* or *alasiw* was established between the two regions.

With spears exchanged, indicating that each region had reviewed its past grievances with the other, the next step in the peace pact procedure is called the *simsim* or *singlip,* the tasting. This is an actual meeting of the leaders from the two regions. Where the meeting takes place depends on the initiative exercised by the proposed peace pact holders. It is not a big affair; the Lubuagan region is said to butcher only a pig for the occasion, but Poswoy informants boast that they always kill a carabao for the event. The *simsim* or *singlip* is a kind of Kalinga powwow where all the grievances discussed by each group separately are now brought out for review by the interregional delegation. If the assembled group appear to find a basis for settling these differences, a date is set for the next meeting or stage in the establishment of a peace pact called the *lonok* or *inom.* The *lonok* or *inom* is a big affair where the issues discussed in the *simsim* or *singlip* are reviewed again and eventually a set of provisions drawn up. At present these provisions are usually written either in Ilocano or English or in both languages, and the set of regulations is designated the *pagta.* The *pagta*—the laws of the *bodong* (peace pact) are to be strictly observed by both regional members.

Let us return again to our hypothetical case:

Upon receiving Emilio's spear, Balniwit has immediately dispatched a messenger to region B inviting Emilio and his regional leaders to the *simsim* or *singlip* in region A. In the meantime Balniwit has contacted the members of his kindred and asked them to contribute food and wine. The meeting is arranged, as is customary, in Balniwit's own hamlet and residence. To impress his visitors, but also his co-regionists, Balniwit has butchered a carabao, arranged for entertainment in the form of a few renditions of Kalinga songs, and has also provided for gong players to furnish music for the dances.

Emilio and his coregionists arrive early on the morning of the first of two days set for the meeting. They are immediately taken to Balniwit's residence where they are given wine while preparation for food and entertainment get underway. Soon the gong players start thumping and dancing begins in front of the residence in a cleared circular area around which stand the regional guests. The visitors from region B are grouped near Balniwit's house and they are asked to begin the dancing. Emilio receives the *ayob* (a piece of cloth) while Balniwit's wife has been given a scarf—both are invitations to dance. Then follow the other male visitors, all of them being matched with region A women. A few women, some of them wives, others relatives of the visitors, have also come and these also dance. The gongs play for about an hour. Then the prominent men from region A deliver speeches of welcome while some chant songs praising the visitors. Some of the visitors, too, deliver speeches complimenting region A for its generous hospitality and fine entertainment. Again the gongs strike up, stopping in about two hours to allow time for the serving of meals on banana leaves spread out on the ground. When everyone has eaten, the gongs play again for about an hour and then stop for the serious discussions to begin. An old man from region A in a faded G-string rises and speaks in a barely audible, raspy voice. He extends a welcome to the visitors, calling them honorable and distinguished guests and praises them for their wisdom and humanitarianism in agreeing to come and help to settle differences between the two regions. He goes on in this vein for about thirty minutes and then gradually moves to citing incidences fostered or perpetrated by region B against his region. He begins with minor offenses—stealing, insults, school fights at Lubuagan—and ends by calling attention to the most grievous of the crimes, the murder of Capitán Y. The old man started out calmly, but ends up shaking with emotion. A middle-aged man in patched tan shorts also from region A speaks from a squatting position on top of a terrace-rock wall. He too praises the intelligence and wisdom of the visitors and moves gradually to the recitation of grievances and like the old man ends up with the murder of Capitán Y. The next speaker is a visitor, incongruous in an old faded corduroy sports jacket and G-string. His voice is loud and controlled, and it is immediately clear that here is a man experienced in oratorical renditions. Chewing betel, he carefully times his most effective remarks with scarlet spittings of betel juice. The visitor speaks for about an hour and a half in praise and flattery, but the final fifteen minutes are devoted to a pointed and remarkably convincing defense of his region, waiving all responsibility of his region in Capitán Y's death. As the visitor finished, a young man in a torn shirt and tattered shorts staggers into the open circle, muttering half-coherent, belligerent remarks. He was a shiftless drunkard from region A and well known as a troublemaker. Balniwit acted quickly and led the drunk out of the cleared area, and at the same time, ordered the musicians to start playing. Thus, a tense moment portending unpleasant consequences was averted by Balniwit's quick thinking and action. In the gaiety of the dancing all is forgotten and when the discussions resume after about an hour, the speaker who answered the visitor's remarks had had a chance to think over his own reply.

This speaker was a school-trained man in his early thirties, a well organized and emphatic speaker, an example of the younger generation with political ambitions who often use peace pact meetings to influence audiences and gather a following. His remarks, delivered in a clear, controlled voice, pointed out the need to settle past grievances to the satisfaction of all concerned and emphasized the importance for the Kalinga to work together and so to reap the benefits that a modern Philippine nation could offer to a united people.

The discussions went on far into the night. As Balniwit sensed a lull in enthusiasm or noted a ruffling of tempers, he would call on the gong players to provide music and thus offer distraction. In the morning, all the issues having been aired and reviewed and a tentative basis reached for their solution, the date for the final stage of the peace pact is set. This final meeting is the *lonok* or *inom* when the *pagta* or law of the *bodong* between regions A and B will be formally drawn and then ratified.

Balniwit once again scored a diplomatic victory by offering his home for the *lonok* celebration. He had cleverly asked prominent coregionists to make appropriate invitational speeches. Overwhelmed by the suddenness of these invitations and perhaps a bit apprehensive that their own region might find it inconvenient to entertain such a large group, the visiting delegation consented to come again to region A for the *lonok*.

Peace pact celebrations, whether renewals, transfers, or simply warm-ups occur during the dry season from March through May. During this time, work in swiddens and fields is at a minimum, the trails are relatively dry, and people have the time to travel and to enjoy the interregional celebrations. It is unlikely, however, that a region will be able to spare the time or to afford to give more than one peace pact feast a year, for these festivals are time consuming and costly. Thus, it is not realistic to assume that the *lonok* which Balniwit had committed his region to celebrate will be given the same year. Since a *lonok* is a big affair to which come not only the people from the two regions involved, but also guests from other regions, a region acting as hosts of a *lonok* will want to prepare for it many weeks ahead of the event.

The description of our hypothetical case may be resumed on the eve of the *lonok*.

Balniwit has put a large number of his kindred to work preparing for the celebration. Some of his relatives have brought large jars of wine, others have prepared sweet cakes of *dikit rice,* and others have furnished rice, coffee, and sugar. Balniwit, himself, has provided two carabaos and three pigs for the feast. Male relatives have worked for more than a week constructing a large pavillion from bamboo poles. Within this structure the main activities of the *lonok* will take place—the review of cases, the drafting of the *pagta,* the dances, and other forms of entertainment. Beyond the dance pavillion leading off from an arbor serving as a temporary kitchen is a long elevated platform underneath a canopy of bamboo poles. This is the dining area; the meals are served on top of the platform out of reach of roaming pigs and dogs. But most impressive of all, thought Balniwit, was a gate archway which he had had constructed at the entrance of his hamlet. On the archway his son had inscribed the words: "Long Live the Peace," "God Bless Us," "Welcome and Mabuhay" (*mabuhay* means welcome in Tagalog). On one end the boy had also drawn a Kalinga headaxe and shield.

Balniwit did not neglect plans for entertainment. He had engaged several orchestras and had organized a number of skits. Women and children were told to practice a version of the song they had sung recently at a *dolnat* (peace pact warm-up) where visitors from region Z had been honored by flowery words incorporated into the chorus. For the *lonok,* region B would be substituted and the song sung at an auspicious moment at the height of the celebration. Chanters of Kalinga songs of praise were also alerted and asked to make especially flattering improvisations in these chants for their guests. Although a song popular in region B was not a favorite in region A, a man from Sumadel recently married into the region and, now a citizen of the region, had been asked to sing a rendition of this song. Finally, Balniwit requested his daughter to repeat the recitation of a poem she had recently recited upon completion of the sixth grade in the central school at Salegseg. The poem was Walt Whitman's on Lincoln, "O Captain, My Captain!", and while Balniwit did not understand the words nor had he ever heard of Lincoln or Walt Whitman, he had been impressed by his daughter's elaborate flourishing hand movements. Pride and strong emotion assailed him as he heard his daughter utter the words "O Captain, My Captain!" (with typical panmontane accent on the final syllable). These designations were, of course, applied among the Kalinga to men of prominence, and while no one as yet had addressed Balniwit as "Captain," he felt that as he gained wealth, prestige, and influence as an arbiter, people would so address him. Yes, it would be most appropriate for his daughter to repeat her recital of "O Captain, My Captain!"

We have attempted in the foregoing hypothetical account to present incidences which were observed in a number of peace pact celebrations and which are typical but which did not all occur in any one specific case.

If we assume that some 300 to 500 people attended the *lonok,* so carefully organized by Balniwit, we have a good notion of the numbers who attend these affairs. The progression of events in the *lonok* follows an order similar to that of the *simsim* or *singlip* already presented in our hypothetical case. A *lonok* is a two-night affair, however. It begins with the arrival of guests early on one morning, goes through that day and night, all of the next day and night, and ends about midmorning of the third day. There are other important differences. The first day and night are devoted to special activities—dancing, singing, and the presentation of skits and plays by children. The serious discussions do not begin until the second day when the provisions of the pact are worked out.

Pact-holders do not ordinarily take part in these discussions, although they may listen occasionally in the role of neutral observers. The visiting pact-holder has the responsibility to watch the behavior of his compatriots to see that they do not do anything to break the good relations between the two groups. The host pact-holder's responsibilities are considerably more involved; he not only has the job of keeping his coregionists in check, which is much more difficult since there are many people from his region attending the event, but he is also responsible for seeing that everything runs smoothly. He must see that there is plenty of wine and food, that important guests receive the special attention they deserve, and most important of all, that his coregionists behave themselves. To neglect any one of these duties will deflate his reputation as a pact-holder and will lower the status of his kinship group and region. If guests are not given deferential treatment, or if a prominent individual is insulted, the incident may bring about the rupture of the pact; certainly it will be one of the cases to be brought up for litigation in a future pact meeting. The Kalinga are extremely sensitive about slights and insults, and demand reparation when they occur.

Entertainment is not prohibited during the *pagta* period of a pact meeting. The host pact-holder observes the lawmakers and if they seem tired, or if heated arguments are under way, he may call for an entertainment diversion. So, periodically, these discussions are interrupted by gong music, by short skits presented by children, and a variety of other types of entertainment. In these interlude periods, a visitor may suddenly arise and give a spontaneous oration, or the pact-holder himself may deliver a speech of admonition. Often a distinguished visitor is asked to speak. If the speaker speaks in English or Ilocano, an interpreter immediately arises and translates the speech into Kalinga.

The proceedings during the *pagta* and the events following may be briefly summarized by reference to a pact meeting between Asiga and Allagigan which I attended in April of 1960. The event took place at Allangigan, Pinokpok municipal district. The lawmakers sat in chairs (rather unusual in orther parts of Kalinga) and discussed the provisions to be incorporated into the *pagta*. The host pact-holder occasionally came to sit and watch, but most of the time he was supervising the distribution of wine, the preparation of food and a host of other tasks. If he noted a lull in the discussions, he often suggested a break for entertainment, which might be dancing, speeches by visitors, or skits presented by children. A rather interesting play was performed during one of these interruptions by the children of a former Ilocano schoolteacher now a retired farmer in a nearby hamlet. The children put on a skit on the life of José Rizal, the Philippine national hero. The part of Rizal was played by the eldest daughter, a teen-age girl who wore slacks, a man's shirt and a black hat for the part. The Kalinga audience was extremely responsive and applauded the performance loudly. I later learned that the play was a stock performance given frequently in Philippine high schools. The incident is noted here to illustrate the varied kinds of entertainment given in peace pact celebrations and also to indicate Kalinga identification with the general Philippine culture as evidenced by their understanding and enthusiastic reception of the play.

In the morning, the *pagta* sessions went on in the manner sketched above. There was a break at midday for meals, eaten off platforms of the type described in the account of the *lonok* given above. In the late afternoon it was announced that the laws of the *pagta* has been drawn to the satisfaction of all the prominent leaders. I was told that later these provisions would be included in the *pagta* portion of the written pact and signed (or marked with an X) by the pact-holders and the prominent men who had participated in the discussions.

Immediately upon announcement that the provisions were accepted, the pact-holders and their wives formed a double line facing each other. They were given a Chinese plate of wine from which all drank in turn until the wine was consumed. Two rice-pounding mortars were then inverted and on each of the mortars a dish of wine was set and two individuals, one from Asiga and one from Allangigan, took turns in drinking the wine. Each person had to drink all the wine without picking up the dish. The dishes were refilled as soon as they were emptied and another pair crouched over the mortar to drink. This wine drinking rite in the

A Kalinga peace pact holder from the Poswoy region (northern Kalinga) with his young son. This is the traditional northern Kalinga men's costume: short jacket, blanket over one shoulder, and an ornamental bag for betel-nut ingredients and other small objects. Men wear the bead necklace as a choker.

lonok is called the *totom*. This went on until all had drunk, whereupon the gong-playing and dancing was resumed. The important part of the peace pact was finished and some people left, but the majority remained for the dancing and entertainment which continued until well past midnight. Toward morning, the *pokaw,* or *palpaliwat* began. These are the boasting sessions of men who have either a headhunting or a war record, or both. The boasts are chanted in a halting voice and made to rhyme. How cleverly a boaster chooses his words and how cleverly he rhymes them reflect credit on him. While the audience seems to enjoy these affairs and the performers have some status among youths, most of the young prominent leaders in the regions I have visited do not participate in the event. It is my belief that as headhunting and killings lose their prestige value, as is happening rapidly, these boasting sessions will disappear.

The *pokaw* sessions terminated the Asiga-Allangigan peace pact celebration and by midmorning of the third day only a few people remained. The Asiga people received gifts of food and items of clothing and departed happily for home. It had been a grand affair and there was time for a few more such celebrations before the heavy rains began. The dry season is presently a gay season for the Kalinga; formerly it was the time for headhunting, but Western contact and influences have brought about important changes, some good, some bad. The peace pact system is considered a good thing by the Kalinga.

If a pact is being newly established, the first step, the exchange of spears, is initiated by two individuals who hope to benefit personally from the arrangement. The advantages that such individuals might hope to enjoy, for example, would be trading privileges, but there may be other benefits as well. The two individuals who initiate the arrangement ordinarily become the pact-holders, but each individual's regional leaders have the authority to choose another person—the one they feel to be the most qualified—to hold the pact. The person they choose must, however, come from the same descent group as the initiator of the pact.

Once a pact has been established and then broken, the new pact-holder (should the original pact-holder have died or resigned, voluntarily or through pressure from regional leaders) is drawn from the descent group of the original holder. Thus, the initial holder of a pact becomes the head of a descent group since all subsequent holders of the pact must be drawn from his bilateral descendents. So far, these descent groups have shallow roots; they go back no more than three or four generations, and of course, new pacts are still being initiated with towns or regions outside the Kalinga subprovince. Peace pacts, the Kalinga say, are inherited like property, but the regional leaders pass it along to the individual of the descent group who they feel is most qualified to hold the pact. Women may also hold pacts, but they do not perform the tasks that are associated with it and a husband or a near relative must act for them. A husband who performs the duties of pact-holder for his wife does not "own" the pact; hence he cannot pass on the pact to members of his own kindred. One of his children by his pact-holder wife may, of course, inherit it and be the pact-holder with approval of regional leaders, but if he marries again, his children by his second wife and their descendents have no right to the pact.

The body of provisions or *pagta* of the peace pact clearly indicates the application of intraregional adjudication procedures to interregional problems. The differences which may be observed in peace pact provisions from one area to another reflect regional and areal variations in custom laws. Close geographical regions employ a large number of designations for custom law procedures in the deliberations during the pagta discussions as well as in the written version of the *pagta*. On the other hand, peace pacts between regions lying at considerable distance from one another try to discuss the laws in more general terms, and the body of provisions contained in the pagta are similarly phrased in general terms.

Some of the terms of litigation and their meanings used in intraregional adjudication procedures are listed below. These designations are now commonly employed in peace pact discussions and deliberations. The terms listed here are specifically from the region of Poswoy, but cognate forms exist in other regions of the Kalinga subprovince.

boto	Payment to those helping to arbitrate or settle a dispute. In the peace pact, *boto* is a fine payable to both peace pact holders.
dalagdag	A counter injury inflicted by one who has been injured or wounded. It may be specified by regional leaders to settle a case of accidental injury.
dosa	Indemnity or wergild to be paid to the relatives of an injured party.
kigad	A sign, usually of knotted runo leaves, marking a regional boundary line alongside a trail.
pasoksok	A bribe made by a thief or offender to one who has caught the culprit in the act of committing a crime with the understanding that the offense will not be reported. The term is also used for a gift of money given to an influential individual to curry favor, like giving money to a judge to dismiss a case.
pasolot or *pasarot*	The return of a stolen article together with another item equal in value.
molta	A fine when the case is settled informally. It defrays the expenses of a feast celebrated to bring the principles of a dispute and their kindred together.
soldak	(Lubuagan *bakdoy*) The declaration of a neutral zone or truce between two regions at war with one another by a third, uninvolved party.

The body of the provisions contained in the *pagta* reflect panmontane principles of kinship and blood feud. For example, in many pacts a killing is not negotiable by fines, but the provisions prescribe satisfaction by payment with another life. In such pacts, the pact-holder from the murderer's region must kill the murderer of someone from the murderer's kindred to keep the pact in force and prevent war or vengeance. Among the Northern Kalinga it is possible to negotiate a killing by payment of *boto* and *dosa*. The former illustrates the old vengeance pattern of "evening the score," while the settlement of homicide by fines appears to be a concession to modern pressures to bring down the incidence of killings and woundings. All regions hold to the traditional view that the kindred is collectively responsible for the act, and conversely that the kindred must share in the wergild and fines when one of its members has been murdered or wounded. Further, accidental homicide or injury is rarely differentiated from intentional killing or wounding. Kindreds bring pressure for satisfaction no matter how an infraction may have been brought about as long as it can somehow be related to another region or kindred. In minor accidental injuries inflicted by another, the practice of token woundings (*dalagdag*) is a technique by which payments of vengeance are avoided, but this is not very common. All of these practices are, of course, features of the kinship principle and the blood feud which are deeply imbedded in Kalinga thinking and which find expression in the pace pact provisions.

Despite the fact that the northern Kalinga regions incorporate a provision to settle homicide with a *dosa,* kindreds are rarely satisfied with simply being paid off, and often retaliate by a counter-killing or wounding. Homicide more than any other act brings about the rupture of a pact, and the pact holder does not always have the courage to take a life from his own region to satisfy the pact provisions in those pacts which give him such a license.

Kalinga peace pact documents which I have examined all have the following general pattern:

1. A statement giving the names of the peace pact holders and their pledge to uphold the provisions of the pact.

2. The specification of the boundaries of the region or towns to be covered by the pact.

3. The *pagta* proper, listing the "laws" or provisions of the pact. Among these, the most common are:

a. *Killing and Wounding:* Specification is made as to whether interregional killings and woundings should be settled by payment of fines and indemnities (*dosa*) or only by counterkillings and token woundings (*dalagdag*). This provision also includes payment of a *boto,* if any, and indicates the amount. The amount of the *dosa* is not ordinarily made in this provision, but is left open for discussion and settlement between the two pact-holders after the act has taken place.

b. *Stealing:* Ordinarily this provision provides for return of the stolen items with another article of equal value (*pasalot* or *pasarot*), or if the stolen item cannot be returned, by a payment twice its value. In some pacts, the amount demanded is triple the value of the article; in this case, one-third goes to the pact-holder and the rest to the person from whom the article was stolen. Payment of this type made to the pact-holder is not considered *boto* as *boto* is conceived to be an offense against the peace pact itself; hence both pact-holders receive a payment. The payment which a peace pact holder receives in adjudicating a case of stealing is a "collector's fee."

c. *Lost Articles:* This provision is sometimes made a part of the article for stealing. The provision provides for the protection of a visitor's property. If an article is lost, and is not found during the immediate search which has been initiated by the pact-holder, the visitor is compensated by money or gifts worth twice the value of the article lost. The compensation is made from a collection made by the pact-holder among his coregionists.

d. *Hospitality:* Hospitality is one of the most important provisions of the peace pact and is included in all the pacts. It guarantees the following accommodations and benefits:

(1) A generous welcome to the visitor,
(2) The best of lodging and food,
(3) Assistance to those who are traders
(4) Help in the collection of debts (if this is the object of the visit).

A northern Kalinga woman photographed at a peace pact meeting. Note typical short jacket, necklace of agate and pottery beads, and the large earplug.

In addition to these main acts, others are usually included to make the visitor as comfortable as possible.

e. *Death, Illness, and Accidents:* This provision assures visitors immediate attention and the best accommodations available in the region in the case of an unfortunate mishap. The provision usually specifies acts as follows: If the visitor is injured or becomes ill, he will be treated according to his wishes or the customs of his region; in the event of death, the body will be wrapped in blankets and quickly dispatched to his home region with some money or a pig to help in the funeral expenses.

f. *Courting Married and Unmarried Women:* Most pacts stipulate the payment of a fine or *boto* by a man who courts or attempts to court a married woman. A husband who will kill or injure the lover, his wife, or both, is not censured. But, such a rule does not apply to a jealous wife who might take vengeance on her husband or his mistress. A wife who kills or wounds either her husband or his mistress becomes subject to the provisions and penalties that govern killings and woundings.

Most pacts under this category or under a specific provision also include a statement which indicates that concubinage is sanctioned as long as the woman enters into the arrangement freely and voluntarily.

The provision about courting an unmarried woman usually states simply that the visitor must make the fact known to the pact-holder for his region.

g. *Respect of Neutrality:* A provision to respect the neutrality (*soldak* or *bakdoy*) of a region is often incorporated into the pact. This means that if regions A and B have a pact, and B is at war with C, members of C must not be harmed by members of B on A's territory. Since most pacts carry this provision, a visitor caught in a region which has just broken its pact with his own may seek refuge in an adjacent region. For a man caught in this predicament, however, the best thing to do is to run to the home of the pact-holder for his region who is obligated to protect him and to have him conducted home safely.

4. *Residence:* Most pacts include a provision which requires that in interregional marriages the regional affiliation of the couple be specifically established. If residence is in a location other than the home region of either one of the couple, protection is facilitated if the couple and their children become citizens of only one region. If the couple decides to establish their residence in the home region of one or the other, the alien spouse must change his or her citizenship.

Dual citizenship is discouraged, for it presents difficulties in enforcing the pact, although the individual who holds it is in an advantageous position. Such an individual receives double protection; should one region of which he is a citizen break its pact with another, he is still covered by the second's pact. But an individual with a "double citizenship" presents too much of a headache to the two pact-holders responsible for him and he is pressured to choose one and drop the other.

5. *Inclusion or exclusion from the pact:* A statement indicating those members of a region to be included or excluded from a pact is an important part of the peace pact document. Students or wage workers usually carry the povisions of the pact wherever they are studying or working, but a colony of a region, such as those of Mabaca in Tabuk, might be excluded. The reason for this exclusion is that a population which is so far removed from the parent region cannot be protected adequately, nor can its members be watched carefully enough to prevent them from breaking the pact. In some pacts, regional members who are government law enforcement officers are specifically exempt from some of the provisions of a pact. Thus, a police officer who kills a member of another region is not liable

(nor is his kindred) to the provision which sanctions a counterkilling, or imposes fines and penalties for homicide.

6. The final part of the peace pact document lists as witnesses of the pact, the signatures, thumb prints or X-marks of the peace pact holders. Underneath the two signatures, arranged in two columns, there are the signatures or marks of some of the prominent men of the two regions. These are the men who have engaged in the discussions and deliberations which have resolved the past grievances and which have resulted in compiling the articles or provisions contained in the *pagta.*

In addition to the general provisions listed above, there are more particular ones in specific pacts. Thus, in a pact between Lubuagan and Sallapadan (Abra), a provision instructs each pact-holder when acting as host to visitors from the other region to keep dogs from barking, to keep down "impolite noises" of regional members while eating, to prevent the rattling of pots and pans in the kitchen, and to control the tempers of men and women in the house. The pact also has a provision directing the pact-holder to see that drunkards do not annoy any visiting members from the other region and authorizes the pact-holder to punish such troublemakers. Some regions also put in a provision for collecting indemnities from a region which has killed or wounded a recent guest. For example, during the period of my research, a lowlander on his way to the Limos region (Pinokpok municipal district) was fed and lodged in Alingag (Salegseg region, Balbalan) and then proceeded to Limos, where he was killed. Salegseg has registered a complaint and a claim for indemnities against Limos for having killed a guest "whose stomach still contained the food served him as a guest of the Salegseg people." A visitor in northern Kalinga remains the guest of the region where he has last eaten, hence the region where he is subsequently killed is obligated to pay indemnities to the region where the victim was a guest.

It is clear from the above account that the Kalinga peace pact system is based on ideas and adjudication procedures already present in the endogamous regional populations. These intraregional, intrakindred techniques for resolving local problems were simply transferred to settle interregional difficulties when mobility became an essential part of Kalinga life. In the transfer, it is apparent the adjudication processes and the character of the pact meetings themselves adhered closely to traditional concepts and practices revolving around the key principles of kinship and the blood feud. While the pacts were made between regions or communities, they are still conceived as pacts between kindreds. Also, retaliation by killing or counter wounding is still sanctioned in most of the pacts for homicide. The pact-holder carries on in only slightly modified form the characteristics of the courageous warrior or *mangol* of headhunting days. Headhunting has almost completely receded into the past and the modern pact-holder need not have a headhunting record, but like the *mangol,* he must be courageous; and if circumstances demand it and in order to keep the peace, he must be willing to kill a member of his own kindred. A weak man cannot be a pact-holder and regional leaders make sure they appoint a strong man as a pact-holder, but always the choice is made from the nearest kin of the initial holder's bilateral descendents.

The peace pact system is thus not a radically new thing to the Kalinga; and because its organization and procedures are familiar, the institution has spread rapidly. Peace pacts are most numerous in the subprovince of Kalinga, but they spill over the boundaries into Abra, the Cagayan valley, and into the adjacent subprovinces of Bontoc and Apayao. Regional populations in the central area, that is, those in the municipal districts of Tinglayan, Lubuagan, Tanudan, and Balbalan rarely have less than fifty pacts with other regions and communities. Pacts are sometimes broken, but so important are they for providing physical security that negotiations for renewal are immediately initiated. The Kalinga peace pact institution serves a highly valued social function as well as a safety one, however. It permits ambitious men to achieve status and distinction beyond regional and community boundaries as wise counselors and arbiters. For the regional populations at large, peace pact meetings provide social interaction and recreation on a grand scale.

6

Social and Cultural Reorganization

WESTERN INFLUENCES and American control redirected Kalinga culture perhaps more profoundly than the cultures of other peoples in the Mountain Province. The initial contact between Americans and Kalinga was friendly. Native leaders and American lieutenant-governors during the first two decades of the present century set about the task of organizing and readjusting social usages on a Western model. It is remarkable how quickly and how smoothly changes were brought about. At the turn of the century, the populations within the present subprovince of Kalinga were restricted to geographical regions; they were feuding, warring, and taking heads across these regional units. Over a period of a half century, a host of changes have taken place: headhunting has virtually stopped; a sense of ethnic oneness has developed; American-type schools have been established; and the Kalinga have become a part of the Philippine local, provincial, and national governmental system fashioned along Spanish and American patterns. The efforts to Christianize the Kalinga may not have developed as rapidly, but it is noteworthy that Belgian and American missionaries have been well received. The changes have come about largely through the efforts of the Kalinga themselves; administrative officials from the outside have been limited.

With the suppression of headhunting, the Kalinga's quest for the satisfaction of personal prestige needs has been directed to positions created by the modern Philippine political and governmental structure and to participation in the popular Kalinga peace pact system. The Kalinga nominate and elect a variety of officers on the local and municipal levels and follow enthusiastically political activities on all levels of the Philippine political hierarchy. Aspirants to political offices or to non-elective positions in the government are not wanting. The drive for individual achievement and distinction, however, is highlighted in the peace pact meetings. In these meetings, the male Kalinga is given full opportunity to exercise his love for debate and oratory. Proud and haughty aspirants for leadership who in former times might simply have taken spear and headaxe to settle an injury, killing, or an insult from a foreign region, now match oratorical wits with one another.

98

The modern courtroom and the clever lawyer trying an infraction of criminal law are mirrored in the peace pact arena. The courtroom is a small vacant plot in a village or under an arbor hastily erected for the occasion. The jury is the assembled audience of a large portion of the two regional populations and visitors from other regions having pacts with the two principal regional participants. The Kalinga speaker may appear insignificant in a G-string or an old pair of faded shorts, tattered and torn, but eloquent words and skillful amassing of evidence against the opposing region evokes respect and admiration from coregionists and opponents alike. There are no formal requirements to practice law and no restriction based on class, caste, or occupation. The ability to persuade and to suggest reasonable forms of arbitration which maintain the honor and dignity of the regional populations measure the stature of the Kalinga arbiter. Such a man now enjoys the status and distinction formerly accorded the renowned headhunter.

Today, there are frequent interactions of Kalinga from different regions and areas, particularly in connection with peace pact meetings. This is the reversal of the process of cultural differentiation which existed during the time of warfare and headhunting. Marriages between formerly endogamous regions are now beginning to take place with attendant cultural exchanges. The Kalinga are now aware of being a distinct people; and while such identity has some political overtones, it is unlikely that this ethnic consciousness will develop into a nationalistic movement. The Kalinga have much in common with other ethnic groups in northern Luzon and through wage work and schools where they are commingled with other mountain peoples, they are now beginning to recognize a common destiny. Kalinga concerns and interests thus go beyond the subprovince to the Mountain Province, and from thence to the Philippine nation and the world.

References

ANDERSON, BARBARA, 1960, in manuscript. "Report on Some Lexico-Statistical Counts on Languages of the Mountain Province, Philippines." University of Chicago Philippine Studies Center.

BARTON, F. R., 1919, *Ifugao Law*. University of California Publications in American Archaeology and Ethnology, Vol. 15.

———, 1946, *The Religion of the Ifugaos*, Memoir 65, American Anthropological Association, 219 pp.

———, 1949, *The Kalingas, Their Institutions and Custom Law*. Chicago: University of Chicago Press.

———, 1955, *The Mythology of the Ifugaos*. Memoirs of the American Folklore Society, Vol. 46. Philadelphia: American Folklore Society.

COLE, F. C., 1915, "Traditions of the Tinguian," in *Anthropological Series*. Chicago: Field Museum of Natural History, Vol. 14, No. 1, Publication 180, pp. 1–226.

———, 1922, "The Tinguian," *Anthropological Series*. Chicago: Field Museum of Natural History, Vol. 14, No. 2, Publication 209, pp. 231–493.

DAVENPORT, WILLIAM, 1959, "Nonunilinear Descent and Descent Groups," *American Anthropologist*, Vol. 61, pp. 557–72.

EGGAN, FRED, 1959, in manuscript. "Ceremonial Organization and Reorganization in Sagada." Chicago: University of Chicago Philippine Studies Center.

———, 1960, "The Sagada Igorots of Northern Luzon," in *Social Structure in Southeast Asia*, G. P. Murdock, ed. Viking Fund Publications in Anthropology, No. 29. Chicago: Quadrangle Books.

FOLKMAR, D., 1906, "Social Institutions of the Tinglayan Igorot." Original manuscript in the H. O. Beyer Collection, Manila. Typescript copies in the University of Chicago Philippine Studies Center.

GOODENOUGH, WARD H., 1955, "A Problem in Malayo—Polynesian Social Organization," *American Anthropologist*, Vol. 57, pp. 71–83.

JENKS, A. E., 1905, *The Bontoc Igorot*. Manila: Philippine Islands Ethnological Survey Publications, Vol. 1.

KEESING, F. M., 1962, *The Ethnohistory of Northern Luzon*. Stanford, Calif.: Stanford University Press.

———, and MARIA KEESING, 1934, *Taming Philippine Headhunters: A Study of Government and of Cultural Change in Northern Luzon*. London: George Allen and Unwin, Ltd.

LAMBRECHT, F., 1953, "Genealogical Trees of Mayawyaw." *Journal of East Asiatic Studies,* Vol. 2, pp. 21–27.

——, 1954. "Genealogical Tree of Kiangan." *Journal of East Asiatic Studies,* Vol. 3, pp. 366–369.

LANDE, CARL H., 1958, *Politics in the Philippines.* Ph.D. Thesis Department of Government, Harvard University, Cambridge, Mass., pp. 1–387.

LEAÑO, ISABEL WALLINGCHAN, 1958, *The Ibaloys of Takdian: Their Social, Economic, and Religious Life.* (Mimeographed.) Graduate School, The Philippine Women's University, Manila.

LOWIE, ROBERT H., 1954, *Indians of the Plains,* American Museum of Natural History, Anthropological Handbooks, No. 1. New York: McGraw-Hill Book Company, Inc.

MINTZ, SIDNEY W. and ERIC R. WOLF, 1950, "An Analysis of Ritual Co-Parenthood (Compadrazgo)," *Southwestern Journal of Anthropology,* Vol. 6, pp. 341–368.

MURDOCK, GEORGE P., 1949, *Social Structure.* New York: Crowell-Collier and Macmillan, Inc.

NADEL, S. F., 1946, "A Study of Shamanism in the Nuba Mountains," *Journal of the Royal Anthropological Institute,* Vol. LXXVI, pp. 25–37.

SCOTT, WILLIAM H., 1958a, "A Preliminary Report on Upland Rice in Northern Luzon," *Southwestern Journal of Anthropology,* Vol. 14, pp. 87–105.

——, 1958b, "Economic and Material Culture of the Kalingas of Madukayan," *Southwestern Journal of Anthropology,* Vol. 14, pp. 318–337.

——, 1960, "The Word Igorot," *Philippine Studies,* Vol. 8, pp. 234–248.

——, 1962, "Cordillera Architecture of Northern Luzon," *Journal of Far Eastern Folklore,* Tokyo. Vol. 21, pp. 186–220.

SCHUSKY, ERNEST L., 1965, *Manual for Kinship Analysis,* Studies in Anthropological Method Series. New York: Holt, Rinehart and Winston, Inc.

SPIER, LESLIE, 1925, "The Distribution of Kinship Systems in North America," *University of Washington Publications in Anthropology,* Vol. 1, No. 2, pp. 71–88.

VANOVERBERGH, M., 1929, *Dress and Adornment in the Mountain Province of Luzon, Philippine Islands.* Publication of the Catholic Anthropological Conference, Vol. 1, pp. 181–242.

VAYDA, ANDREW P., 1961, "Expansion and Warfare Among Swidden Agriculturists," *American Anthropologist,* Vol. 63, pp. 346–358.

WORCESTER, DEAN C., 1912, "Head-hunters of Northern Luzon." *National Geographic,* Vol. 23, pp. 833–930.

——, 1913, "The Non-Christian Tribes of the Philippines," *National Geographic,* Vol. 24, pp. 1157–1256.

——, and R. HAYDEN, 1930, *The Philippines Past and Present.* New York: Crowell-Collier and Macmillan, Inc.

Recommended Reading

BARTON, F. R., 1919, *Ifugao Law,* University of California Publications in American Archaeology and Ethnology, Vol. 15. A classic work on the law-ways of a central Mountain Province people. Some of the legal procedures and concepts of the Ifugao are similar to those of the Kalinga described in the present case study.

————, 1949, *The Kalingas.* Chicago: University of Chicago Press. A study of the Kalinga wet-rice cultivators of Lubuagan. This study, together with those of William H. Scott and the author, afford good comparative material for understanding the general patterns of Kalinga life.

DeRAEDT, JULES, 1964 C.I.C.M. Religious Representations in Northern Luzon. *Saint Louis Quarterly,* Baguio City, Philippines. Vol. 2, No. 3, pp. 245–348. In a historical comparative study, Father DeRaedt analyzes the religious expressions of the Mountain Province peoples and demonstrates the correlation between ecological and subsistence practices and religious representations.

DOZIER, EDWARD P., 1966, *Mountain Arbiters—The Changing Life of a Philippine Hill People.* Tuscon, Ariz.: University of Arizona Press. This is a study primarily of the Northern Kalinga, but provides as well comparative notes from Luguagan and other southern Kalinga areas.

KEESING, FELIX M., 1962, *The Ethnohistory of Northern Luzon.* Stanford, Calif.: Stanford University Press. Published posthumously, this study analyzes the ethnohistorical materials bearing on the Mountain Peoples and their immediate neighbors. Keesing's work is imperative for an understanding of the historical roots of the peoples in northern Luzon.

SCOTT, WILLIAM H., 1958a, "A Preliminary Report on Upland Rice in Northern Luzon," *Southwestern Journal of Anthropology,* Vol. 14, pp. 87–105. Scott's investigations indicate that irrigated-rice techniques have diffused northward from the central Bontoc area either displacing dry or upland rice or seriously competing with the latter type of cultivation. Material cultural items from the Bontoc area have also diffused along with the expansion of irrigated rice.

————, 1958b, "Economic and Material Culture of the Kalingas of Madukayan," *Southwestern Journal of Anthropology,* Vol. 14, pp. 318–337. Scott's article is the only account that deals with an Eastern Kalinga cultural group. The report is restricted to a description of the economic and material cultural phenomena. It is clear that close affinities in these patterns exist between both the Southern and Northern Kalinga.

WORCESTER, DEAN C., and R. HAYDEN, 1930, *The Philippines Past and Present.* New York: Crowell-Collier and Macmillan, Inc. Chapters on the Mountain Province describe the first American encounters with the Kalinga. Excellent data on the relations of early American administrators and the mountain peoples of Northern Luzon.